C000163223

# Discovering
# Highwaymen

SHIRE PUBLICATIONS LTD

Published in 1994 by Shire Publications Ltd, Cromwell House, Church Street, Princes Risborough, Buckinghamshire HP27 9AA, UK.

Copyright © 1970 and 1994 by Russell Ash. First published 1970; second, expanded edition 1994. Number 94 in the Discovering series. ISBN 0 7478 0260 2.

Printed in Great Britain by CIT Printing Services, Press Buildings, Merlins Bridge, Haverfordwest, Dyfed SA61 1XF.

British Library Cataloguing in Publication Data: Ash, Russell. Discovering Highwaymen. – 2 Rev. ed.– (Discovering series; No. 94). I. Title. II. Series. 364. 1552. ISBN 0-7478-0260-2.

Cover illustration: *The legend that Claude Duval allowed a lady to keep her jewels when she danced with him on Hounslow Heath is the subject of the painting 'Claude Duval' by William Powell Frith, a detail of which is reproduced.* © Manchester City Art Galleries.

# CONTENTS

*Walter Stanley Paget's ironically titled 'The Good Old Times' depicts something of the terror of highway robbery.*

# 1

# THE AGE OF HIGHWAYMEN

The daring hold-ups and amazing exploits of many highwaymen made them heroes in their lifetime and legends in ours. Their deeds were commemorated in the popular literature of the seventeenth and eighteenth centuries, and their hangings attracted immense crowds. This notoriety was not without foundation as some were just as we imagine them – fearless cavaliers; carefree chivalrous romantic knights in periwigs, masks and three-cornered hats; adventurers, often of noble birth – true 'Gentlemen of the Road'. Yet many more, such as the half-mythical Dick Turpin, were unmitigated and ungallant rogues who simply desired easy money, caring little for the consequences – which usually included death at an early age.

There have been robbers on the highway as long as roads have been in existence, but the archetypal hero/villain appeared early in the seventeenth century. He was a well-known character by the late 1640s, in the last days of Charles I, and became an established stereotype during the Commonwealth (1649–60). In this period the highwayman fraternity included many passionate Royalists who declared that they robbed only the followers of Cromwell. They caused so much trouble to the Rump Parliament that Lord Fairfax issued a Proclamation (17 September 1649) offering £10 reward for the capture of any highwayman ('the State's Officers exempted', as the Royalists satirically commented). On 28 December 1649, at Tyburn, the main venue for executions in London, twenty-seven men were hanged for offences that included highway robbery. Captain Reynolds, the most notorious of all, cried from the scaffold, 'God bless King Charles – Vive le Roi!'

These recalcitrants continued to operate even after the Civil War. The disbandment of large numbers of soldiers led to massive unemployment, and many took to the road for their livelihoods out of sheer necessity. They were joined by all manner of men with a variety of reasons for choosing this particular profession.

Impoverished gamblers, for example, frequently held up more fortunate ones. As early as 1617, William Fenner had aptly noted in a pamphlet that Tyburn Tree and Wapping Gibbets had 'many hangers-on' recruited from the ranks of these broken gamesters.

There were also servants who desired the ways of their masters, but lacked more honest means of obtaining them, and gay young blades who robbed on the highway, or 'High Toby', for the sheer excitement of it.

Many highwaymen were well educated, like Augustine King, described in a 1687 advertisement in the *London Gazette* as 'a lusty fat man'. He was a graduate of King's College, Cambridge, who met his end on the gallows in 1688. 'Young Gentleman Harry' – Harry Simms – was, he said, an Old Etonian, and a notorious highwayman to boot. He was captured at Dunstable and hanged at Tyburn in June 1747 after a prosperous and dashing career.

Many more had good backgrounds. Gamaliel Ratsey was the son of a gentleman of Market Deeping in Lincolnshire. He received a good education and had a distinguished career in the army, but on his return to England he became a highwayman and committed numerous robberies in the Spalding area. He wore a hideous mask to terrorise his victims (and thus was nicknamed 'Gamaliel Hobgoblin'), and prior to his execution at Bedford (26 March 1605) he had escaped from jail wearing only a shirt. There is a story that he once robbed an actor, from whom he first demanded a speech from the newly performed *Hamlet*, and on another occasion he forced a scholar to deliver a learned thesis. Sir Josselin Denville, similarly, once compelled a monk to preach a sermon in praise of theft.

Some highwaymen were the sons of parsons. James Maclaine's father was an Irish Presbyterian minister, and Nicholas Horner, hanged at Exeter in 1719, was the son of the vicar of Honiton. Paul Lewis, hanged at Tyburn, was the son of a clergyman of Herstmonceux in Sussex.

Many highwaymen followed respectable trades, either before taking to the road, or as 'covers' during their criminal careers. William Davis, the so-called 'Golden Farmer', was indeed a well-respected farmer, and one Clibborn was believed to be an honest baker until he was killed while committing a savage robbery. John Cottington, a Royalist highwayman, had been a chimney sweep and is represented in popular prints with his brushes over his shoulder.

Some highwaymen were high-born, like William Parsons, whose father was a baronet, and his aunt the Duchess of Northumberland. He incurred gambling debts after his expulsion from Eton, became a highwayman, and was captured on Hounslow Heath and hanged at Tyburn in 1751. Usually though, influential or aristocratic connections worked wonders. Morgan, described as 'an amateur highwayman', was reprieved as the cart drew up to the gallows, while his friends and accomplices, Brett, Whalley and Dupree, were hanged. All came from good families, but Morgan had the additional advantage of being engaged to Lady Elizabeth Hamilton whose pleadings led to his life being spared by the king. Sir Simon Clarke, Bart., operated with a Lieutenant Arnott in Hampshire

*William Hogarth's 'Ruin'd at a Gaming Table' identifies a common route into highway robbery among young blades.*

until he was captured and tried at Winchester. The fears of the High Sheriff over the threatened scandal resulted in the petitioning of the king and his subsequent reprieve.

Bribery and corruption also secured the release of many a highwayman. 'He can't be hanged who hath Five Hundred Pounds at his command', wrote the robber Francis Jackson. Minor legal technicalities, too, often conveniently ended the trials of obviously guilty men with their dismissal, and there were many flagrant breaches of legal procedure. Two highwaymen, Everett and Williams, who operated on Finchley Common and elsewhere, planned to split the £2,000 which they stole. Williams, however, declined to give Everett his share. Everett, with immense audacity, then sued him. The whole affair ended with Everett paying costs and the lawyers being fined £50 each for their parts in such an outrageous suit.

## Methods of operation

The methods of most highwaymen did not attain great levels of sophistication, and 'your-money-or-your-life' and a gun in the ribs usually achieved the desired result. William Davis, it is said, lured unsuspecting travellers to lonely spots by riding with them for miles, chatting casually, before launching sudden and violent attacks on them. William Page was more subtle, and used detailed road maps and wore cunning disguises. After robberies, he would change clothes and ride away in an unsuspicious coach and pair. Tom Collet disguised himself as a bishop, and Tom Rowland and Tom Sympson dressed as women while Mary Frith, known as Moll Cutpurse, a pickpocket and one-time highwaywoman, dressed as a man. James Maclaine wore a dramatic Venetian mask, but generally the most they did was to stuff the tails of their wigs into their mouths to obscure part of the face. Most notorious highwaymen were well described in advertisements of the period and apparently made no attempt to disguise themselves or to change their habits or horses. In his *Recantation*, published in 1674, the retired highwayman Francis Jackson outlined the methods used by highwaymen, giving instructions on their recognition, the avoidance of robbery and action to be taken in the event of hold-ups. His advice was necessary as this was a lawless age and highway robbery was commonplace.

The writer Horace Walpole – himself a victim of a hold-up by a highwayman – stated that one was '…forced to travel even at noon as if one was going into battle'. But this was only one of many aspects of the lawlessness. Young blades killed their servants, or each other, in duels and their crimes were lightly regarded, whilst a man who stole a watch, if caught, would almost certainly be hanged.

## Mail robbery

In the pre-coaching days, young postboys were employed who were so vulnerable to attack that at one time the Post Office advised the public to send banknotes in two halves, and to wait for news of the safe arrival of the first half before forwarding the second.

In 1796 it was recommended that the very young boys should be replaced by those over 18 and under 45 years of age, and that they should be issued with two pistols, swords and protective helmets, but the great expense of this proposal was prohibitive, and it was never carried out.

In the early 1800s, after several years with few robberies, a new wave began, and highwaymen employed obstructions such as felled trees to stop mail coaches. There were numerous incidents in which guards fought off attackers with their blunderbusses and rewards of up to £50 were offered to those assisting in the conviction of mail robbers.

As the railways appeared, however, and as police methods improved, mail robbery gradually became a very rare occurrence.

See here the Preſideſſe o'th pilfring Trade
Mercuryes ſecond; Venus's onely Mayd
Doublet and breeches in a Un'form dreſſe
The Female Humuriſt a Kickſhaw meſſe
Heres no attraction that your fancy greets
But if her FEATURES pleaſe not read her FEATS..

*Highwaywoman Mary Frith, known as 'Moll Cutpurse', was the heroine of Middleton and Dekker's 1611 play 'The Roaring Girle'.*

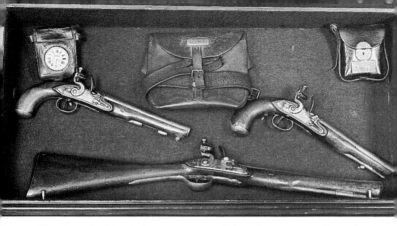

*Pistols and a blunderbuss were essential equipment on mail coaches.*

## Measures taken against highwaymen

The theft of any article worth more than a shilling was once a capital offence. Even into the nineteenth century there were over two hundred offences for which one could, technically, be hanged, though in fact only about twenty-five of these were generally considered worthy of the maximum penalty.

Henry Fielding, the novelist and author of *Tom Jones*, was a vociferous opponent of the law's disparities and the flagrant and unchecked breaches of it. He thought it '...high time to put a stop to the further progress of such impudent and audacious insults'. He put much blame on the effects of the cheap gin which was obtainable almost everywhere and which appeared to be the staple diet of large numbers of people, and the desire for easy money and quick rises in station by what he termed 'the dregs of the people'. Fielding also opposed gambling and spectacular public hangings in which the criminal was made into a hero by the mob, making speeches from the scaffold while his 'dying confessions' were being sold to the rapacious crowd, having been ghost-written and printed hours before.

These hangings certainly did not appear to deter would-be highway robbers, who became an ever greater menace in the eighteenth century. In the absence of an effective police force the unlucky traveller had recourse only to the 'hundred', the area where the robbery had been committed. César de Saussure, the Swiss traveller, wrote of what he regarded as 'a queer law' in the early eighteenth century:

'If a man is robbed of a considerable sum in the daytime and on the high road, and if he declares his loss to the Sheriff of the county before the sun sets, and can prove that the sum has been

10

taken from him in such and such a place, the county is obliged to refund him the sum.'

The Hundred of Benhurst in Berkshire had repeatedly to pay travellers for losses incurred along the Bath Road through Maidenhead Thicket, a notorious spot for robberies. In 1585 an Act of Parliament limited the sum recoverable from the Hundred to half the loss, but in 1590 Benhurst had still to pay out the then large sum of £255 in compensation. The Sunday Trading Act of 1676 made sure that anyone foolish enough to travel in the hours of darkness or on Sunday must be prepared to suffer the consequences, and during these excluded periods the Hundred was not responsible for repayment of losses.

Quite apart from robbery, it was still quite possible to be murdered by robbers while travelling in England in the late eighteenth and early nineteenth centuries. Largely, however highwaymen – who considered themselves the 'aristocrats of criminals' – were generally polite and non-violent unless provoked. Many foreign travellers in particular noted this fact and contrasted it with the behaviour of murderous brigands on the Continent.

The peak of the highwayman era was 1650 to 1750. The highways were being used more and more, but they were badly constructed and maintained and were made doubly dangerous by highwaymen lurking in the lonely areas that bordered main roads well into the nineteenth century. In fact, it has been said that the age of highwaymen did not completely end until that of the railways began. The bridle paths and minor roads – the 'Low Toby' – and the streets of towns were also hazardous and were infested with footpads, unable to operate on the highway where they were no match for mounted men or travellers in coaches.

The collective responsibility of the hundreds and counties continued throughout this period, and there were various isolated attempts at ridding notorious areas of the dangers of highwaymen. In 1722 turnpike men on the Shoreditch/Cheshunt road (now the A10) were issued with speaking trumpets in an effort to warn travellers of the prevalence of highwaymen. It is uncertain how this worked, and whether the turnpike men were expected to wander up and down the road shouting 'Beware of Highwaymen!', but apparently it was effective, and there were no robberies on this stretch of road for several years.

## The thief-takers

'Highwaymen becoming, some time after the Revolution, exceedingly bold and troublesome, by an Act made in the reign of William and Mary, a reward of forty pounds is given for apprehending any one in England or Wales, and prosecuting him so as he be convicted; which forty pounds is to be paid by the sheriff on a certificate of the judge or justices before whom such a felon was convicted. And in case a person shall be killed in endeavouring to apprehend or making pursuit after such robbers, the said forty pounds shall be paid to the executors or administrators of such persons upon the like certificate. Moreover, every person who shall take, apprehend, or convict such a person, shall have as a reward the horse, furniture, arms, money or other goods of such robber as shall be taken with him, the right or title of his Majesty's bodies politic or corporate, lords of manors, or persons lending or letting the same such robber notwithstanding; excepting only the right of those from whom such horses, furniture, arms, money, or goods were before feloniously taken.'

*Lives of the Most Remarkable Criminals*, 1735

Following the passing of this Act, a class of professional bounty-hunters, or 'thief-takers', promptly appeared, chief of whom was Jonathan Wild, 'Thief-Taker General of Great Britain and Ireland', who sent over sixty criminals to the gallows. He also ran a profitable protection racket for criminals but was himself hanged in 1725. Some thief-takers also operated as *agents provocateurs*, encouraging common thieves to become highwaymen in order to secure the additional rewards for their eventual capture. The rewards to thief-takers rose greatly during the eighteenth century, but meanwhile superior methods of crime prevention and the capture of criminals were being developed by Henry and John Fielding. Henry became Bow Street magistrate, probably the first uncorrupt person to hold that office. He was assisted by his blind half-brother, John, and by the Duke of Newcastle. With meagre government financial backing they set about their enormous task of establishing a workable police system. The word 'police' had been used in England as early as 1714, but the establishment of a force had long been resisted by those who feared infringements on their liberty. In 1751 Henry Fielding published his *Inquiry into the Causes of the Late Increase of Robbers*, which prompted certain reforms, but he died in Lisbon in 1754. John took charge at Bow Street from 1761 to 1780. In 1755 he had published his *Plan for Preventing Robberies within Twenty Miles of London* and attempted to encourage the payment of messengers to report crimes immediately. He worked under great difficulties and had to overcome resistance from all quarters. He had even to issue itemised invoices for work done, such as, in 1756: 'Pursuing and apprehending Jonathan Wigmore, highwayman, for attempting to rob the King of Poland's groom, £8 8s.'

In 1761, a civilian horse patrol was established to safeguard

*Blind judge Sir John Fielding, founder of the Bow Street Runners, began a vigorous campaign against highway robbery.*

roads on the outskirts of London. It was disbanded and re-formed several times well into the nineteenth century, by which time highway robbery was showing signs of a considerable decline. Horse patrols were still required in some parts of the country, however, and as late as 1807 a highwayman called Allen was shot by the militia near Midhurst, thus ending his career of robbery on the road between Arundel and Chichester.

The philosopher Edmund Burke, who died in 1797, stated that the age of highwaymen was over, and that the age of cheats had begun; but he was a little premature. In Wiltshire, at Fisherton

13

Gaol, Salisbury, alone, between 1806 and 1824, six highwaymen were hanged, and in 1839 three were sent for fifteen years' transportation for robbery at Gore Cross on Salisbury Plain.

The death penalty for all but murder and attempted murder was ended in 1838, after which there was a tendency for transportation, rather than imprisonment, to take its place, although as early as 1666 an Act had been passed that offered transportation to the American colonies as an alternative to hanging in certain cases.

By the beginning of the nineteenth century there was an increasing trend towards the use of banks, and cheques were used to make payments of large sums of money. A measure restricting cash payments came into force in 1797 and made pickings less attractive to highway robbers.

The ostler in George Borrow's *The Romany Rye* (1857) states that the decline of highway robbery was due to the refusal of the authorities to license those inns that were known haunts of highwaymen, to the enclosure of the heathland where they traditionally lay in wait for travellers, and to the establishment of a well-armed mounted patrol on the roads out of London. Jerry Abershaw, who was hanged in 1795, was the last really famous highwayman, and by the 1830s highway robbery had become something of a rarity.

# 2

# ROUTES AND ROBBERIES

In the age of highwaymen no traveller was really safe anywhere. It was as dangerous in busy towns as on deserted country roads, and a nobleman with an escort was as susceptible to attack and robbery as a man journeying alone, but certain areas attracted special reputations.

## London

'4 May 1674: Between 7 & 8 aclock, 5 or more horsmen dogd ye Duke of Ormond, who went home by ye way of Pal-mal & soe up James' Street & just as his coach came to ye upper end thereof, one of them clapt a pistoll to his coachman that if eyther he spoke or drove he was a dead man, the rest alighted & comanded him out of ye coach; he told them that if it were his money they should have it, soe they puld him out of ye coach, forct him on horsback behind one of them, & away they carried him, my Ld havinge recollected himself that he had gone about 30 paces as he ghessed (& as he told me himself for I went yesterday morninge to see him) & finding he was hinmost, his foreman havinge his sword & bridle in one hand, & his pistoll in ye other wrested ye pistoll out of his hand, & threw ye fellow downe, fell with him & upon him, & gott his sword & gott loose of them not with out some other hazards one pistoll beinge shott att him & two more fired. He is bruised in his ey, & a knock over the pate with a pistoll as he ghessed, & a small cutt in his head, after all which he is like I thank God to doe well. This makes all ye towne wonder, if money had beene their designe they might have had it, if his life, they might have had it alsoe. Some think & conjecture only, that their malice & spite was such that they would have carried him to Tiburne, & have hanged him there. They cannot Imagine whom to suspect for it. The horse they left behind. It was a chestnutt, with a bald face, & a white spott on his side. He that was dismounted gott off in ye dark & crowd.'

'1679: A couple of highwaymen having robbed a countryman & leaving him his horse, he pursued 'em with a hue & cry which overtook them, but they being very stout fought their way through Islington & all the road along to this town's end, where after both their swords were broke in their hands & they unhorsed, they were seized & carried to Newgate. 'Tis great pity such men should be hanged.'

John Verney, *Memoirs of the Verney Family*

As the capital and richest city in the kingdom, London particularly attracted highwaymen, who found concealment easy in the metropolis. Francis Jackson noted that a man might lose himself in London, where strangers attracted little attention. There was also much traffic on which to prey and, as there were numerous 'fences', the disposal of stolen goods presented no problem. Many used the city as a base from which to ride forth, rob and return to hide in one of the several notorious areas such as Clare Market near Aldwych.

Some did not even trouble to leave the town to commit their robberies. The Duchess of Montrose was robbed by a highwayman as she was carried across Bond Street in a sedan chair, and in 1726 the Earl of Harborough was robbed in Piccadilly in mid-morning.

In his diary Horace Walpole noted the frequency of robberies in London and wrote of an incident which occurred one Sunday night in September 1750 whilst he was sitting in the dining room of his house in Arlington Street. He heard the cry 'Stop Thief!' in the street below. A postchaise had been stopped and robbed at the corner of Arlington Street and Piccadilly and an unfortunate watchman had been knocked to the ground as the highwayman made his escape.

In 1768, a highwayman, having committed a robbery in Piccadilly, escaped from his pursuers by riding up Berkeley Street and down Lansdowne Passage, which then divided the gardens of Lansdowne House and the Duke of Devonshire's town-house. He rode into Bolton Street and away into the night. To prevent similar escapes, an iron bar was placed at the entrance to the passage.

Robberies in London persisted for many years. Even King George II was robbed by an apologetic highwayman who climbed the wall of his garden at Kensington. John Fielding had commenced his work of suppressing highway robbery in London in the 1750s by such brusque means as organising surprise raids on masquerade balls where male guests were hustled into the gaming rooms, unmasked and compelled to give accounts of their movements. By these and more conventional methods, the menace of highway robbery within London was slowly reduced.

Out of London, however, all were easy prey to highwaymen in an age when one could travel for hours even on a main road without sighting habitation. According to the economist Josiah Tucker in his *The Elements of Commerce* (1755), the heaths outside London could '...answer no other end but to be a Rendezvous for Highwaymen and a commodious scene for them to exercise their Profession'.

Along these dangerous routes in the pre-railway era journeyed many wealthy men – merchants, farmers, and members of the court – and in the days before the use of banks became general there was a good chance of their carrying large sums of money. Of course, there were more roads serving London than any other part of the country, and certain of these roads became notorious for the risks attached to travelling along them.

## The Dover Road

This, now the A2, was one of the most dangerous roads. Gad's Hill, near Rochester, acquired an early reputation, and the Gravesend registers have many references to thieves and travellers alike being killed on this stretch of road as early as the 1500s. Shakespeare made the highway near Gad's Hill the setting for the robbery by Sir John Falstaff and Prince Hal in *Henry IV Part I* (Act II Scene 2). In 1656 the Danish Ambassador was robbed there, but the Duke of Wurtemberg was luckier, and narrowly escaped robbery by driving furiously when a man with a drawn sword appeared in the path of his coach. Daniel Defoe observed that Gad's Hill was dangerous because highwaymen lurked there to rob seamen who had received their pay at Chatham and were on their way to London to spend it.

Shooters Hill, Woolwich, was similarly notorious. *The Times* of 2 January 1798 reported an incident that had occurred on the evening of the previous Sunday, 30 December 1797, when a postchaise carrying two lawyers, Harrison and Lockhart, and a midshipman from HMS *Venerable* was stopped by highwaymen as it travelled from London to Sheerness: 'The man on Mr Harrison's side treated him with much personal violence, by forcing his pistol into his mouth, on opening the chaise door', and the unfortunate midshipman had his trunk, which contained all his clothes, stolen.

The Bull Inn, at the crest of Shooters Hill, was, in coaching times, the first post house at which travellers stopped to change horses on the road from London. Like many inns, it is said to have been used by Dick Turpin. Shooters Hill was also a popular place for hanging and gibbeting robbers, especially on the tall gibbets which once stood beside the Eltham Road. Samuel Pepys wrote in his *Diary* on 11 April 1661 that he had journeyed along the Dover Road 'under the man that hangs upon Shooters Hill, and a filthy sight it is to see how his flesh is shrunk to his bones'.

## The Bath Road

The Bath Road, now the A4, was dangerous because robbers were especially on the look-out for wealthy men and members of court as they drove down to fashionable Bath to 'partake of the mineral waters'. The *London Gazette* of 1 December 1681 contained a typical report of an incident:

'Robb'd the 10th of Nov. last, from Mr Joseph Bullock of Bristol, on the Road between Hungerford and Newbury in Barkshire, one Silver Watch and Case, there being on the backside of the Case an Almanack, a Hanger with a Plate Hilt, a Buff Belt, with Silver Buckles; by Three Men, the one a middle-sized Man, full Fac'd, a short White Wigg much Curl'd in an old Cloth-colour riding Coat, on a Fleabitten Horse, about 14 hands high, his Brows Brown; the other a middle-sized Black-Favour'd, on a Grey Horse, above 14 hands high, with Black Hair, or Wigg, and thin Favour, the other a full set Man, thin Favour'd with curled dark Brown Hair. Whoever can discover the Persons aforesaid to Mr Bullock of Bristol or at the Three Cups in Breadstreet, London (the said Robbers having killed one John Thomas, the said Mr Bullock's Servant) shall have their Charges and ten pounds reward.'

(The almost incidental reference to the murder of John Thomas is a revealing indication of the relative values placed on servants and on property in these lawless times.)

Knightsbridge and Kensington in this period lay well outside the built-up part of London and were particularly notorious. John Evelyn noted in his diaries the prevalence of robberies on this stretch of road in the seventeenth century (for example, under the cover of a dense fog in November 1699), and the burial register of St Mary Abbot's Church, Kensington, shows that on 29 November 1687 Thomas Ridge of Portsmouth was 'killed by thieves almost at Knightsbridge'. On 1 July 1744, William Hawkes, one of several known as 'The Flying Highwaymen' (Thomas Boulter, hanged in 1778, was another), was hanged for robberies committed there.

On 3 June 1752, Norton, a professional thief-taker, apprehended William Belcher, a highwayman who had robbed the Devizes Chaise, by himself riding in a chaise to Halfway House, an inn between Knightsbridge and Kensington, and seizing Belcher when he attempted a hold-up.

At one time in the eighteenth century, at Kensington, a bell was rung at intervals on Sunday evenings to muster people returning to London who, for safety, travelled only when a fair-sized group had assembled. As late as 1798 a highwayman haunted Knightsbridge and robbed coaches that stuck in the mud where a small stream from Hyde Park ran across the road.

Hounslow Heath was an especially unpleasant area – a wasteland haunted by highwaymen such as Claude Duval in the time of Charles II. Two main roads crossed the heath – the Bath Road (A4) from Hounslow to Colnbrook, and the Exeter Road (A30) to

*The Bell Inn in Hounslow stands where the Bath Road started across Hounslow Heath.*

Staines. The Bath Road was also the road to Windsor, where the Court was held, and was therefore used by many wealthy travellers. The Duke of Northumberland was attacked by highwaymen and robbed, but some like Lord Ossulton in 1698 escaped, as did the Duke of St Albans, who, with the aid of his companions, beat off their assailants. In the eighteenth century, a square brick building was erected by the Bath Road at Gunnersbury between St James's church and Gunnersbury Lane to provide shelter for the king's horse patrol that rode out to guard the road when the king and his court travelled between London and Windsor.

There is a story that Twysden, Bishop of Raphoe in Donegal, a man of Kentish descent, died after being shot under circumstances that suggested his operating as a highwayman on the Heath.

The fifth Earl of Berkeley had a seat at Crawford Park on Hounslow Heath, where he used to stay for long weekends. He had been stopped by highwaymen more than once and took to riding about heavily armed. Once, when an obviously lone highwayman

19

attacked his coach, he distracted him by telling him that his companion was clearly visible behind him. As the robber turned his head, the Earl shot him dead. He also killed Cran Jones, another highwayman, setting his clothes ablaze with a close-range shot.

## The Great North Road

This, the present A1, might well be called Dick Turpin's Road, judging from the astonishing number of robberies he is said to have committed on it. Finchley Common was a favourite haunt of his as well as of many other highwaymen. William Cady terrorised the Common for four years but was captured and hanged at Tyburn in 1687 for the murder of a groom. On 11 July 1699, Captain Edmund Tool, or Tooley, and his gang attacked Robert Leader on the Common. They stripped and robbed him and his servant. Leader attempted to escape but was shot in the back and died the next day. Tool was subsequently arrested at the Blue Ball in Jermyn Street and executed on 2 February 1700, after which his body was hanged in chains on Finchley Common – a well-known location for gibbeting the bodies of malefactors.

Jack Sheppard, although best remembered as a master prison escaper, had a short career as a highwayman, ending with his capture on Finchley Common on 10 September 1724.

The Common remained dangerous until the nineteenth century. The Earl of Minto, travelling to London in 1790, wrote to his wife: 'I shall not trust my throat on Finchley Common in the dark.'

## The Oxford Road

Like the other roads out of London, the Oxford Road (A40) had its dangerous and its relatively safe stretches. It was said that once past Hillingdon one was pretty secure until Shotover Hill near Oxford, but a story is told that in the woodland between West Wycombe and Stokenchurch Jack Shrimpton, the highwayman, met a barrister who admired Shrimpton's horse and offered him £30 for it. Shrimpton, it is related, received the cash but the barrister did not get the horse. Apart from this amusing incident, Shrimpton went on to pursue an unsuccessful career and was eventually hanged on St Michael's Hill, Bristol, on 4 September 1713.

## West Country roads

The West Country roads, especially those crossing Salisbury Plain, were extremely hazardous in the eighteenth century. A broadside (the not altogether trustworthy popular press of the day) of 1712 tells how Nat Seager, riding from Shaftesbury to Blandford Forum, was robbed and wounded by a highwayman who then

*The Bull on the Oxford Road at Gerrards Cross was supposedly a haunt of the local highwayman Jack Shrimpton.*

galloped off. Soon, Joseph Reader, a powerfully built miller of Shaftesbury, came across Seager who told him what had occurred. Reader promptly borrowed Seager's horse and overtook the highwayman, who fired two pistols at him, both of which missed. Reader then overpowered him, beating him with a club. Seager by this time had followed on foot and was sent off for assistance. Reader, perhaps fearing the loss of the customary £40 reward should the robber escape, hanged him from a tree using his own belt. Seager then arrived with the Sheriff, who arrested Reader, charging him with the murder of the highwayman. He was tried at Dorchester Assizes but, after some stern words from the judge, was acquitted and rewarded for his resourcefulness.

Serjeant Merewether, who defended a member of the Cherhill gang which operated in the Marlborough, Calne and Devizes area, was robbed of his fee by his client on his way home. Another member of the gang, which infested the Bath Road for years, used to leap out upon travellers stark naked, scaring them into parting with their money and valuables.

A newspaper report of January 1743, shows that chivalry and fair play were not lacking in this part of the world:

'A Captain of the army, who was going to Bath in a post-chaise, was stopped near Sandy Lane by two highwaymen, by one of whom he was told that he wanted but a guinea, which he hoped to be soon able to pay him again. The Captain gave him a guinea,

21

and the fellow gave the driver a shilling, and told the gentleman if he was stopped by any one else, to say 'Virgin Mary', that being the watchword for the day. They had not gone far before they were stopped by four persons – but on being given the watchword, they raised their hats, and rode off.'

## North of London

Especially during the reigns of James I and Charles II, the road to Newmarket was a well-known place for hold-ups of gamblers and members of the Court. The Newmarket Road became so bad that *The Domestic Intelligence* of 24 August 1617 reported a pitched battle in that month between highwaymen and outraged locals in which five highwaymen were wounded and one killed.

An audacious group of ex-soldiers, after their disbandment in 1698, set up a 'Highwayman Colony' in Epping Forest near Waltham Cross and held up travellers on the Cambridge and Newmarket Roads. A raid directed by the Lord Chief Justice broke them up, but they re-formed, sending a letter of defiance to the Government. A detachment of dragoons was then sent out, and the colony permanently destroyed.

North of London, many headline-hitting robberies took place from time to time. The notorious Bracy gang, which also broke into houses, operating in the 1670s, took £1,800 from a wagon which they held up near Newark.

In November 1692, highwaymen robbed the Manchester Carrier of £15,000 tax money at South Mimms as it drove between St Albans and London under escort. The raid was carried out with great precision and, like others where large hauls were involved, may have been a politically inspired plot. The incident was described by the diarist John Evelyn:

'A signal Robbery of the Tax mony brought out of the North Country towards Lond; set upon by severall desperat persons, who dismounted & stopt all Travellers on the Rode, & guarding them in a field, when the exploit was don, & The Treasure taken, killed all the Horses of those they had stay'd, to hinder the pursuit of them; 16 horses they stabbed & then dismis'd those that they had dismounted.'

In November 1692, highwaymen captured between £1,500 and £2,000 from a wagon near Barnet. This was an outstanding incident in a series of robberies that ended with an encounter on 6 December 1692, between dragoons sent out to suppress the robberies and the band of highwaymen led by Captain James Whitney. One dragoon was killed, but Whitney was captured and executed.

The *Birmingham Gazette* of 6 May 1751 reported that, travelling between the Green Dragon at Hatherton, and the Welsh Harp at

GENERAL POST-OFFICE,
*Monday, May 18, 1801.*

THE Post-boy, conveying the Mail from Tring to Hemel Hempstead, was stopped near Bonrd, in the Parish of North Church, about Fifn Minutes past Ten o'Clock last Night, by a gle Highwayman, mounted upon a dark-coured grey Horse, who took from him the followg Bags of Letters for London, viz.

| | |
|---|---|
| Winslow, | |
| Wendover, | |
| Aylesbury, | Bags for London. |
| Tring, and | |
| Birkhampstead | |

There is great Reason to suspect that one James ook committed this Robbery. He is a Native Hungerford, where his Father now resides,—between 30 and 40 Years of Age, about 5 Feet or 11 Inches high, has light brown Hair cut ort, is pitted with the Small-pox, has lived in d about Mary-le-bone, for Five or Six Years il, and is well known in the Neighbourhood of rtland-place. He left his Lodgings at No. 3, Woodstock-street, Mary-le-bone, early on Satury Morning, and was then dressed in a blue at, with black Velvet Collar, Marcella Waistut, with blue and white Stripes, Velveteen reeches, and dark-coloured Stockings. He was ied at the Old Bailey, about a Year ago, for se-stealing, and acquitted. He is supposed to ve in his Possession several Bank of England tes, Aylesbury, High Wycomb, Uxbridge, ney Stratford, and Banbury Notes.

Whoever shall apprehend and convict, or cause be apprehended and convicted, the Person who mitted the said Robbery, will be entitled to a eward of TWO HUNDRED POUNDS, er and above the Reward given by Act of Parament for apprehending Highwaymen: Or if ny Person concerned therein will surrender himf, and make Discovery, whereby the Person who mitted the Robbery may be apprehended and ought to Justice, such Discoverer will be enitled to the said Reward, and will also receive s Majesty's most gracious Pardon

By Command of his Majesty's Post-master General,

FRANCIS FREELING, Secretary.

*The London Chronicle of 19-21 May 1801 reports the attack by James (alias Robert) Snook or Snooks on a post-boy, with the announcement of an unusually large reward for his capture.*

*Below is Snooks's grave on Boxmoor Common, Hertfordshire. Hanging was the usual penalty for mail robbery, for which Snooks was executed in 1802.*

Stonnal, a coach had been stopped and robbed on 30 April by a solitary highwayman who behaved very civilly to the passengers and requested their 'assistance' in his distress, although he politely refused coppers, saying he never took them. He then escorted the coach for some distance down the road.

There is a touching story recounted in the *Morning Chronicle* of 14 January 1797 of a chivalrous highwayman who declined to steal a ring belonging to a lady whose coach he had stopped, when she told him 'she would sooner part with life' – the sort of tale that helped to establish the myth of the universal gallantry of 'gentlemen of the road', thereby ensuring them a place in history that in most instances was undeserved.

# 3

# THE END OF THE ROAD

## Newgate and St Sepulchre
All you that in the condemned hole do lie,
Prepare you, for tomorrow you shall die.
Watch all and pray the hour is drawing near
That you before the Almighty must appear.
Examine well yourselves. In time repent
That you may not to eternal flames be sent.
And when St Sepulchre's bell tomorrow tolls
The Lord have mercy on your souls.
*Solemn Exhortation to condemned prisoners in Newgate Prison*

In spite of the inefficiency of the system of bringing criminals to justice, a surprising number of murderers, coiners, highwaymen and other criminals eventually found themselves in Newgate, for long the chief criminal prison of the town and county of London. It was named after a gate with a small prison attached at the present site of the Old Bailey. One of the many prisons that occupied the same site was built in 1086 by the Bishop of London and was used to imprison persons of rank as early as 1218. The administrators of the will of Lord Mayor Richard Whittington, famed as 'Dick Whittington', who died in 1423, had it rebuilt to his instructions; it was later rebuilt again and a statue of Whittington and his equally famous cat stood in a niche there until the destruction of the prison in the Great Fire of 1666. It was rebuilt by 1672 but pulled down and rebuilt again in 1778–80. During the Gordon Riots of 1780, the interior was gutted by fire and restored. It ceased to be used as a debtors' prison in 1815 and after 1849 was used only to house prisoners awaiting trial. In 1857 the interior was rebuilt on the reformatory plan but it fell gradually into disuse after the Prison Bill of 1877. By the end of 1881 its function had been taken over by Pentonville and other new London prisons. It was demolished in 1902–3 and the present Central Criminal Court (the Old Bailey) stands on its site.

Newgate was appallingly squalid, filthy and disease-ridden. The drinking water was drawn from a spring which received the over-flow of a nearby cesspool, and on one occasion two judges, the Lord Mayor and sixty jurymen, witnesses and attendants died of typhus in the adjoining Sessions House. Jailfever was rampant, and the air so foul that many were rendered unconscious by it.

*'Clever Tom Clinch', the subject of Swift's poem, is represented on one of a set of cigarette cards of pirates and highwaymen issued by Lambert & Butler in 1926.*

Some prisoners were left there for years on end, heavily manacled and in disgusting conditions. If they had a little money they could bribe their keepers into allowing them 'easement of irons', and if they had a lot of money they could rent 'apartments' off the Press Yard – an exercise yard where prisoners were tortured by having heavy weights placed on their chests until they either died or pleaded as required.

Many notorious prisoners received guests in their cells. William Hawkes, 'The Flying Highwayman', was condemned in July 1744, after an outstanding career. Many distinguished persons visited him in his cell, including Lord George Hanger, later the fourth Lord Coleraine, who, delighted by Hawkes's wit, offered him £50 to use as bribes to escape. The plan failed, and Hawkes was hanged, his body afterwards being laid to rest in Stepney church-yard with the epitaph: 'Fairewell, vain world, I've had enough of thee.'

The site of Newgate is commemorated by a plaque on the wall of the Old Bailey in Newgate Street, which reads, rather inaccurately: 'Site of Newgate. Demolished 1777.'

In 1605, the no doubt well-meaning Robert Dowe, a citizen of London and Merchant Taylor, left a bequest of £50 to the Vicar and Churchwarden of the Church of the Holy Sepulchre without Newgate, known as St Sepulchre, for the reciting of a 'solemn exhortation delivered with an audible voice' to the condemned criminals in Newgate at midnight on the eve of their execution. Dramatic emphasis was added by the ringing of the 'execution bell'. The bellman was to 'give twelve solemn towles with double strokes', and those present were called to '...pray heartily unto God, for those Poor sinners, who are now going to their deaths, for whom this great bell doth toll'. The vicar was evidently not to be trusted, and the beadle of Merchant Taylors' Hall was also given a 'modest stipend' to ensure that this task was carried out. As time went by, the watchmen took over the exhortation, which took the form of a melodramatic poem. The practice was noted by John Webster in his *The Duchess of Malfi*, which he wrote in 1612–13:

I am the common bellman
That usually is sent to condemned prisoners
The night before they die.

The midnight bellman ceased in 1783, but the bell was rung on execution mornings until 1890. The bellman used a tunnel which led from St Sepulchre to outside the condemned cells until 1868. The entrance in the church is now bricked up but may still be seen. The bell is also in St Sepulchre in a glass case with the full lines of the exhortation on a brass plaque in the case.

## Hangman's Highway

As clever Tom Clinch, while the rabble was bawling,
Rode stately through Holborn to die at his calling,
He stopt at the 'Bowl' for a bottle of sack,
And promised to pay for it when he came back.
His waistcoat and stockings and breeches were white;
His cap had a new cherry ribbon to tie't.
The maids to the doors and balconies ran,
And said, 'Lack-a-day, he's a proper young man!'
But, as from the windows the ladies he spied,
Like a beau in the box, he bow'd low on each side!

And when his last speech the loud hawkers did cry
He swore from his cart 'It was all a damn'd lie!'
The hangman for pardon fell down on his knee;
Tom gave him a kick in the guts for his fee:
Then said, 'I must speak to the people a little;
But I'll see you all damn'd before I will wittle...
Take courage, dear comrades, and be not afraid,
Nor slip this occasion to follow your trade;
My conscience is clear, and my spirits are calm,
And thus I go off without prayer-book or psalm;
Then follow the practice of Clever Tom Clinch
Who hung like a hero who never would flinch.

Jonathan Swift, *Clever Tom Clinch Going to be Hanged*, 1727

The condemned men usually left Newgate in the early morning in a cart, though 'some gentlemen obtain leave to perform this journey in a coach' (François Misson, the French traveller, writing in 1698). They were accompanied by other felons, as many as twenty or more being hanged in one day – and by their own coffins, if they were lucky enough to escape gibbeting or dissection. Many had prepared themselves with new clothes in the latest style, but the more pessimistic donned shrouds. Often they already wore their nooses tied round their necks.

The journey from Newgate to Tyburn, a distance of about three miles, could take over two hours if the crowds were large. Samuel Richardson, in his *Familiar Letters* of 1741, wrote of a typical execution day, or 'Tyburn Fair', when 'All the way up to Holborn the crowd was so great as at every twenty or thirty yards to obstruct the passage.'

The 'melancholy cavalcade from Newgate to the fatal Tree' stopped almost immediately at the porch of St Sepulchre, where the prisoners received nosegays from the clergyman. The cart then moved off westwards down into the valley of the Fleet River, down Snow Hill and up Heavy (Holborn) Hill, a route now ironed out by Holborn Viaduct across Farringdon Street, which follows the line of the valley.

The procession left the City of London at Holborn Bars, named after the toll-bars on each side of the road at Staple Inn at the bottom of Gray's Inn Road. The old gabled buildings still stand at Staple Inn, near Chancery Lane underground station, and two posts with the arms of the City mark the sites of the original bars. The toll-bars marked the extent of the seventeenth-century City, beyond which there was little development until the eighteenth century. Great Turnstile is a reminder that the area west of Lincoln's Inn was once a meadow. Kingsway is relatively new (1903)

*Staple Inn, Holborn, once a landmark on the route from the City of London to Tyburn.*

and follows what was a narrow lane called Little Queen Street.

The cart proceeded along Holborn, High Holborn and St Giles High Street. The reason for this southward curve in the route is that the area now occupied by New Oxford Street was an unpleasant marshy area known as 'Rugmere', long a slum, and little development took place until the street was built in 1847.

This stretch of the journey was halfway house, and the cart generally stopped to allow its occupants to have a last drink at the Bowl at the corner of Endell Street and Broad Street (now Shaftesbury Avenue). Although the Bowl is mentioned by name in Swift's poem *Clever Tom Clinch*, the White Hart, Drury Lane, and the Three Tuns, South Portman Mews, have both been cited as stopping places for the execution cart. Whichever hostelry was used, according to Samuel Richardson, 'wine, notwithstanding the late good order against this practice, was brought to the malefac-

29

*The White Hart, Drury Lane, one of several claimants as a halt on the road to Tyburn.*

tors, who drank greedily of it'. Many drank so greedily that they were obviously blind drunk by the time they reached Tyburn.

The cart then resumed its journey, crossing the junction of Tottenham Court Road and Charing Cross Road and continuing a straight course down Oxford Street, popularly known as Tyburn Way until about 1718. No houses were built on the north side until the 1720s and the Welsh writer Thomas Pennant (1726–98) remembered it as 'a deep hollow road, and full of sloughs; with here and there a ragged house, the lurking-place of cut-throats.'

However, by 1725, much of the parish of St George, Hanover Square, had been built up and soon became fashionable, a development that later contributed to the ending of public hangings at Tyburn.

## Tyburn Tree

'Hanging is the most common Punishment in England. Usually this Execution is done in a great Road a quarter of a League from the Suburbs of London. The Sessions for trying Criminals being held but Eight Times a Year, there are sometimes twenty Malefactors to be hang'd at a time.'

François Misson, 1698

In the 1780s nearly one hundred criminals were hanged annually in London and Middlesex alone. Between 1749 and 1771, 251 highwaymen were hanged at Tyburn alone, apart from the hundreds of other thieves, murderers and other felons. Hanging was the usual penalty for those convicted of highway robbery until replaced by transportation.

Tyburn was the name given to the area at the junction of the present Bayswater Road, Edgware Road and Oxford Street, now known as Marble Arch. The actual site of the gallows is marked by a circular plaque set into the traffic island at the bottom of Edgware Road, reading 'The Site of Tyburn Tree'.

From Norman times, executions had been held in London at Tyburn and other locations. The Elms opposite St Bartholomew's Hospital was a much used site. John Cottington was hanged at

*The site of Britain's most famous gallows is now a traffic island.*

Smithfield Rounds in 1659, and as late as 1693 Captain James Whitney was executed at Porter's Block near Cowcross Street, Smithfield. Confusingly, Tyburn was also once known as The Elms. The name, Tyburn, comes from the 'Tye Bourne' – the two streams – flowing from Hampstead Heights to the Thames. The West Bourne is commemorated in such names Westbourne Grove. From June 1571 (when John Story became its first victim), Tyburn gallows was a three-legged structure, often called the Triple Tree, standing with one leg in each of the three adjoining parishes of St George Hanover Square, St Marylebone and Paddington.

A hanging day was a public holiday – which was officially encouraged in the hope that the executions would act as a deterrent to would-be malefactors. However, one visitor, a Scottish clergyman, spoke for many when he expressed his belief that the opposite effect resulted:

'Among the immense multitude of spectators, some at windows, some upon carts, thousands standing and jostling one another in the surrounding fields – my conviction is that, in a moral view, a great number were made worse, instead of better, by the awful spectacle. Of the ragamuffin class a large proportion were gratified by the sight; and within my hearing many expressed their admiration of the fortitude, as they termed the hardness and stupidity, of one of the sufferers.'

In his 1751 *Inquiry into the Causes of the Late Increase of Robbers*, Henry Fielding considered that:

'The day appointed by law for the thief's shame is the day of glory in his own opinion. His procession to Tyburn and his last moments there are all triumphant; attended with the compassion of the weak and tender-hearted, and with the applause, admiration and envy of all the bold and hardened.'

Hangings acquired a carnival atmosphere, with vendors of gingerbread, gin and oranges, chapbook sellers, sideshows and pickpockets, a rumbustious scene graphically depicted by William Hogarth in an engraving in his 1747 *Industry and Idleness* series.

The crowds, which could number as many as 200,000 – as they did for the execution of Jack Sheppard – would build up from early morning to a huge throng. Some were lucky enough to secure grandstand seats, as described by the antiquarian John Timbs:

'Around the gibbet were erected open galleries, like a racecourse stand, wherein seats were let to spectators at executions; the key of one of them was kept by Mammy Douglas, 'the Tyburn pew-opener'. In 1758 when Dr Henesey was to have been executed for treason, the prices of seats rose to 2s. and 2s. 6d. – but the doctor being most "provokingly reprieved" a riot ensued and most of the seats were destroyed.'

*A satirical 'invitation' to the hanging of 'Thief-Taker General'*
*Jonathan Wild at Tyburn in 1725.*

On arrival at the gallows, the prisoners would often make speeches to the assembled multitude, as related by François Misson:

'Generally he studies a speech which he pronounces under the gallows, and gives in writing to the sheriff or the minister that attends him in his last moments, desiring that it may be printed.'

Then the chaplain would attempt to prepare the condemned man for his death, though as often as not, according to Samuel Richardson, 'the clergyman who attended was more the subject of ridicule than of serious attention'. His presence was so resented by Isaac Atkinson, a well-educated highwayman, that he stabbed the chaplain on the way to the gallows. Drunken hangmen were also known to have attempted to string up the chaplains who accompanied the prisoners on to the scaffold. There the chaplain would often note the 'last dying confession' for future publication. It is said that while the chaplain ministered to Jonathan Wild, the condemned thief-taker picked his pocket, removing a corkscrew and testifying to the habits of the clergyman by dying with it still clutched in his hand.

Occasionally, prisoners went berserk as they approached the gallows. John Ashton leaped about and announced that he was the Duke of Wellington. As the rope pulled tight, he catapulted back on to the platform and had to be hanged again.

Often a condemned man would die bravely, dropping his handkerchief to signal that he was ready for the drop, though at least once the hangman ruined the effect by rushing forward to grab the handkerchief, which was regarded as his property, before proceeding with the hanging.

One technique of hanging was described by Misson:

'The executioner stops the cart under one of the cross beams of the gibbet, and fastens to that ill-favoured beam one end of the rope, while the other is wound round the wretch's neck. This done, he gives the horses a lash with his whip, away goes the cart, and there swings my gentleman kicking in the air. The hangman does not give himself the trouble to put them out of their pain but some of their friends or relations do it for them. They pull the dying person by the legs and beat his breast to dispatch him as soon as possible.'

Sometimes friends of the hanging man would pull his legs to make the end come quickly, but lightweight men were occasionally only half hanged and subsequently revived by their companions.

As soon as it was apparent that the man was dead carrier pigeons were dispatched with the news to Newgate, while in the crowd, noted Samuel Richardson, 'The face of every one spoke a kind of mirth, as if the spectacle they had beheld had afforded pleasure instead of pain, which I am wholly unable to account for.'

Afterwards, the body was taken away for burial or gibbeting, or conveyed to Surgeons' Hall for dissection; the corpses of executed criminals were especially sought by medical students in the period before the Anatomy Act of 1832 legalised dissection. Even this might not mark the end of the highwayman's useful career, for at one time there was a bizarre practice of using the skin of executed criminals to bind books – most ironically of all, accounts of their own lives. One such example is James Allen's *Narrative of the Life of James Allen, alias George Walton, alias Jonas Pierce, alias James H. York, alias Burley Grove, the Highwayman, being his Death-bed Confession to the Warden of the Massachusetts State Prison,* published in Boston, Massachusetts, by Harrington & Co in 1837. Allen had died in jail while serving a 22-year sentence from robbing James Fenno – and requested that after his death a copy of his books should be bound in his own skin and presented to Mr Fenno. A binder called Peter Low duly carried out the grisly task, and this unique edition is now in the collection of the Boston Athenaeum. (While no known examples of similar works employing the skins of British highwaymen are known, Bristol Royal Infirmary has a copy of surgeon Richard Smith's account of his dismemberment of one John Horwood, the murderer of Eliza Balsam, for which he was hanged on Friday 13 April 1821, bound in his own skin, and the Albert Memorial Library, Exeter, has a copy of Milton's *Poetical Works* bound in the skin of George Cudmore, executed in Devon in 1830 for the murder of his wife, Grace.)

Failing this, as Richardson reported of one grim occasion, the corpse might be unceremoniously abandoned: '...they immediately hawked it about to every surgeon they could think of; and when none would buy it they rubbed tar all over it, and left it in a field scarcely covered with earth.'

In the second half of the eighteenth century, the permanent gallows at Tyburn became an obstruction to traffic as buildings were erected on the fringes of the area, by now known as Oxford Street, after Edward Harley, the second Earl of Oxford, who owned land on the north side. As busy thoroughfares appeared, so temporary gallows were set up nearby when required. The gallows also began to cause offence in this now fashionable residential area. According to the *London Gazette* of 4 May 1771, Lady Waldegrave was having a 'grand house built near Tyburn', and 'through the particular interest of her ladyship, the place of execution will be moved to another spot.'

Consequently, temporary gallows were erected in the area to the west of the old site. A toll house stood on the former site of the

*A gatepost from one of the former Tyburn toll gates is displayed in the window of Lloyds Bank, 195 Edgware Road.*

permanent gallows from about 1760 to 1829, and a stone gatepost from one of the three toll gates is now set in the window of Lloyds Bank at 195 Edgware Road, with a commemorative plaque.

Despite loud protests from Dr Johnson and other advocates of Tyburn public hangings, the last execution took place on 7 November 1783. John Austin, a murderer, was the last occupant of the movable gallows, which were then sawn up and made into stands for beer-butts in the nearby Carpenters Arms public house.

Public hangings continued outside the Old Bailey, though of course without the drama of a journey through the streets of London beforehand. Michael Barrett was the last person to be hanged publicly (for his part in the murder of twelve local inhabitants as a result of the Fenian bomb attack on Clerkenwell Prison) on 26 May 1868. Three days later the Capital Punishment Within Prisons Bill came into force and put an end to the age of spectacular hangings.

## Gibbeting

...they kill'd him,
they kill'd him for robbing the mail.
They hang'd him in chains for a show.

Alfred Tennyson, *Rizpah*, 1880

Most highwaymen regarded it as inevitable that they should end their days on the gallows; but their greatest fear was that their bodies should afterwards fall into the hands of the surgeons for dissection, or, perhaps worst of all, that they should be gibbeted. This meant hanging in irons, sometimes for years, in some desolate spot, an object of curiosity, an alleged deterrent to others, with a risk of being mutilated by the superstitious and by the weather, and with little hope of ever being buried in hallowed ground.

Robbers of the mails were always hanged on conviction, and as a result of the demands of the Earl of Leicester, then Postmaster General, gibbeting was legalised in 1752, and the bodies of hanged mail robbers were thenceforth invariably exhibited hanging in chains.

Gibbeting of criminals by way of example had been practised for many years, however, and continued until 1834 when it was abolished by statute.

As early as 1675, in his *Britannia*, a traveller's 'Book of Roads', the Scottish topographer John Ogilby bore witness to the number of gibbets in England by employing frequent reference to them as landmarks, since they were often situated in high or lonely places. In 1791 William Lewin, hanged at Chester for robbing the mail, was gibbeted at Helsby Tor, where his body could be seen from several counties.

Frequently occult practitioners would remove parts of the decomposing bodies. The hair and teeth were used in potions and remedies, and the hands were particular favourites for making 'hands of glory'. These were used in witchcraft rituals, as described by Thomas Ingoldsby in *The Nurse's Story – The Hand of Glory*:

37

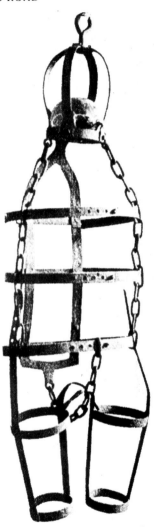

*This set of gibbet irons from Rye contains a grisly relic – the skull of a butcher named Breeds, who in 1742 was hanged and gibbeted for stabbing the town's mayor.*

Now mount who list, And close by the wrist
Sever me quickly the Dead Man's fist! –
Now climb who dare, where he swings in air,
And pluck me five locks of the Dead Man's hair!

Often, too, friends or relatives of the victim would steal the body by night and bury it in a secret place. William Cole, in an eighteenth century history of Cambridge, describes how the younger of the two sons of Mrs Gatward, who kept the Red Lion at Royston in Hertfordshire, robbed the postboy between Royston and Huntingdon. For this crime he was hanged and his body gibbeted at Caxton. After two or three months the gibbet irons collapsed in a strong wind, and a Mr Lord who was passing by observed that the boy's body was quite dried out. As a memento he removed a brass button from the scarlet coat which it still wore. Later Mrs Gatward took the remains to her inn and buried them in the cellar. The story is very similar to that related in Tennyson's *Rizpah*, but it is said that his inspiration for this poem came from seeing the gibbet on the downs between Brighton and Worthing.

To prevent the removal of bodies, the gibbet posts sometimes had spikes driven into them, or were covered with tar. However, a friend of three highwaymen who were gibbeted at the summit of the Chevin in Derbyshire for holding up the mail at Hazelwood

*Caxton Gibbet: a replica of the original gibbet on which the remains of mail-robber Gatward and other highwaymen were displayed.*

was able to set light to the tar-covered post and remains, and thereby put an end to the shameful spectacle. Similarly, several members of the notorious Cherhill gang of West Country highwaymen were hanged at Devizes and their bodies gibbeted on the high ground between Beckhampton and Cherhill on the Bath Road. Surviving members of the gang, resenting this treatment, removed the corpses of their friends for burial and destroyed some of the gibbets. The authorities eventually had the remaining posts iron-bound and covered with nails to deter climbers.

Some dreadful stories are told about gibbets. It is said that John Whitfield was gibbeted alive at Wetheral, Cumbria. He hung in agony for some time until a passing coachman took pity on him and ended his misery by shooting him

Between the Staines Road (A315) and Bath Road (A4) out of Hounslow there once stood a line of gibbets which was a popular spot with tourists on Sundays. The gibbet stumps were discovered in 1899 when the road was being excavated for tramways.

James Cook, a murderer, was the last person to be gibbeted in England. After being hanged at Leicester Prison on 10 August 1832, he was hanged in chains from a huge gibbet at Aylestone. Gibbeting was abolished two years later.

A set of gibbet irons may be seen at Warrington Museum. They were last used on Edward Miles, executed on 14 September 1793 for robbing the mail and murdering the postboy James Hogworth. His body was gibbeted near the Twystes on the road to Manchester and swung there for years. The iron frame was subsequently buried at the foot of the gibbet post, but dug up in 1845.

On the A14, south of the roundabout crossing with the A45 between St Neots and Cambridge, there is a place known as Caxton Gibbet – the spot where young Gatward was hanged and where a gibbet post stood from 1346 or earlier until 1753. A gibbet post (or, more accurately, a copy of one, made in 1934) stands outside the Gibbet Inn, an awful warning or, as a contemporary account puts it: '...a dreadful memento to youth, how they swerve from the paths of rectitude, and transgress the laws of their country' (*The Salisbury Journal*, 25 August 1783).

## Legends, inns and relics

The lives of highwaymen have captured the imagination of all generations since the seventeenth century. Many, rightly or wrongly, have been regarded as Robin Hoods, notable for their chivalry and expertise with horses, guns and women. Their lives were closely followed in contemporary newspapers, and accounts of their lives and confessions in broadsheets and chapbooks, the popular literature of the period, were bestsellers in their day. The

*Intended as a dire warning to would-be criminals, the gibbets on Hounslow Heath became a popular tourist attraction.*

*The highwayman Captain Macheath is reproached by Polly Peachum and Lucy Lockitt in a scene from John Gay's 'The Beggar's Opera'. Premiered in 1728, it did much to enhance the image of the 'gentleman of the road'.*

'Ordinaries', or chaplains of Newgate, frequently corrupt and debauched men, made large sums of money by using their positions of trust to write and sell these accounts of the lives and dying speeches of condemned men, often embroidering them with imaginative fiction.

These pamphlets were the sensational press of the age and, in the days before laws of copyright, were plagiarised all over the country. James Catnach, a printer of these works in the early nineteenth century, sold as many as half a million 'blood-and-thunder' booklets about a single murder and received payment in such vast quantities of pennies that he paved his kitchen with dud coins, purifying the filthy coppers by boiling them in potash and vinegar in great vats.

Larger productions such as the *Newgate Calendars*, the *Tyburn Chronicle* and *Terrific Register*, and Captain Alexander Smith's *Lives of the Highwaymen* of 1714, ran into several editions, but cannot be regarded as serious accounts as they showed little concern for accuracy of detail.

The free-living, rebelliousness and astounding capabilities of highwaymen, occasionally true, but more often alleged, have made fictional heroes out of villains from earliest times. John Gay's *Beggar's Opera* of 1728 made Captain Macheath, a highwayman, its hero. It was immensely popular both as an opera and in book form, but there is strong evidence that it had an adverse effect on the youth of the day, and there were attempts both to reduce the glorification of Macheath and to ban it altogether. It was written at the suggestion of Jonathan Swift, whose own satirical poem about a romantic highwayman, Tom Clinch, was based on the life of a real robber called Thomas Cox.

Perhaps the greatest romanticising of highwaymen of all time was *Rookwood* (1834) by William Harrison Ainsworth. It described the exploits of Dick Turpin and accredited him with the famous ride to York. Even Ainsworth himself was surprised by its phenomenal success, and many subsequent writers have come to regard the parts dealing with Turpin (who is only a secondary

*Popular novelist William Harrison Ainsworth glamorised both Dick Turpin and Jack Sheppard.*

43

*An illustration by George Cruikshank in Ainsworth's 'Rookwood' portrays the death of Turpin's famed, but fictitious, horse Black Bess.*

character) as factual. According to Lord Macaulay, the ride to York legend had been accredited to different men in different generations: Turpin just happened to be the character identified with the story in the early eighteenth century.

'Dick Turpin's Ride' was celebrated in a poem of this title by Alfred Noyes, who, like Ainsworth, helped to perpetuate the myths and legends surrounding highwaymen. There have been thousands of 'lives', ballads, poems and novels based on real and imaginary highwaymen, and even today films continue the story. Dick Turpin has been the subject of more than a dozen films, including, in 1925, a silent one incongruously starring Tom Mix, best-known for his cowboy roles, and on British television was the hero of a series starring Richard O'Sullivan. Jack Sheppard was played in the 1969 film *Where's Jack?* by Tommy Steele (who distorted history by escaping the hangman's noose). Laurence Olivier appeared as Macheath in a 1953 film of *The Beggar's Opera*, and highwaymen (and highwaywomen) were the central characters in *The Wicked Lady* (1945), starring Margaret Lockwood and James Mason, and the 1983 Michael Winner remake starring Alan Bates and with Faye Dunaway in the title role.

Reference is made elsewhere to inns known to have been used by highwaymen. Unfortunately, many taverns with genuine associations have long since been pulled down, and many without authentic claims have constructed them. The number in particular which allege some connection with Dick Turpin is immense. Stewart Marsh Ellis, William Harrison Ainsworth's biographer, travelled along the mythical route of the London to York ride at the beginning of the twentieth century and found an inn or some other relic employing Turpin's name in every village along the road. Turpin would have had to have been a very long-lived alcoholic to have had both time and the inclination to have visited all the pubs which he is said to have drunk or hidden in. He must also have been extremely absent-minded, if the number of guns and other personal effects he left behind is anything to go by.

On the other hand, there were many inns and, especially in the eighteenth century, many highwaymen in England, and there are few inns of any antiquity that do not have some genuine connection with some highwayman, but many commercially (or, to give them the benefit of the doubt, romantically) minded landlords have sought to play on legends with little or no foundation on fact. To give a list of phoneys would give offence to many publicans, while a guide to genuine ones might imply that those not included had fictitious claims for a place in history. Best, therefore, that those who want their beliefs to continue should do so, leaving others to undertake the detective work involved in uncovering examples of bogus 'highwaymen's inns'.

Similarly, highwaymen usually led short lives and 'travelled light'. In consequence, they had little in the way of material possessions. Only seldom is a relic discovered to have an authentic connection with a highwayman. A curator of the York Castle Museum commented that 'the number of stocking purses reputed to have been carried by Turpin would fit out a centipede' and that the leg irons in the museum which most 'authorities' state to have been used on Turpin and Nevison have no certain association with either highwayman.

Sadly too, outlaws are seldom commemorated by those authorities that erect plaques to the memory of more law-abiding persons. According to Charles Harper, a prolific writer on roads and author of a large work on highwaymen, '...the shrines of saints and the haunts of the highwaymen are alike the food of ravenous Time.'

There are few memorials to highwaymen, and even identifiable graves are rare and epitaphs rarer, although one punning example comes from Nayland in Suffolk:

Edward Alston 1760
Here sleeps in dust
Ned Alston
The notorious Essex highwayman
Ob. Anno Dom: 1760
Aetat. 40

My friend, here I am - Death has at last prevailed,
And for once all my projects are baffled.
'Tis a blessing to know, though, when once a man's nailed,
He no longer has fear of the scaffold.
My life was cut short by a shot through the head
On his Majesty's highway at Dalston;
So now 'Number One's' numbered one of the dead
All's one if he's Alston or all-stone.

More commonly they were often buried without ceremony, or, as malefactors, dissected by surgeons or gibbeted until all that remained were a few bleached bones and a few tattered bits of cloth, so that in most cases, only their memory survives.

# 4

# HEROES AND VILLAINS

**Jerry Abershaw *c*.1773–95**

**He died with his boots *off*.**

Although he had only a short career, the name of Louis Jeremiah Avershawe, known as Jerry Abershaw, soon became synonymous with any daring robbery.

He was born at Kingston in Surrey, and although very little is known of his early life, we do know that his mother soon became aware of her son's criminal instincts and assured him that he would die with his boots on.

He became a highwayman at the age of about seventeen and was soon the leader of a notorious gang which terrorised the roads between London and the Kingston and Wimbledon area, using the Bald-Faced Stag at Kingston as their headquarters, despite the protests of the landlord. There is a story that a Dr William Rootes of Putney was called to attend to Abershaw when he took ill at this inn. Quite unaware of the identity of his patient, he declined the offer of an escort back to his home, declaring that he feared no one, 'Not even Abershaw himself!'

Jerry Abershaw also frequented a house in Clerkenwell known as the Old House in West Street, and at one time notorious for its many sliding doors and secret passages, much used by such villains as Jonathan Wild and Jack Sheppard.

Toward the end of his short, though prosperous, career, an attempt was made to arrest Abershaw at the Three Brewers in Southwark, in January 1795. He managed to escape, firing off two pistols, killing David Price, one of the Bow Street Runners, with one shot, and wounding the landlord, Bernard Turner, with the other. He was subsequently captured, however, and tried at Croydon Assizes on 30 July 1795, for the murder of the peace officer. A legal technicality invalidated this charge, but he was sentenced to death, found guilty of felonious shooting. Abershaw was disdainful of the court's proceedings, donning his own hat as the judge assumed the black cap to pronounce sentence and 'observing him with contemptuous looks'. He became quite riotous in the court,

*Jerry's Hill, between Putney and Wimbledon, where Jerry Abershaw's body was gibbeted.*

and had to be dragged from it heavily manacled. Imprisoned in Newgate, he drew sketches depicting his exploits on the white walls of his cell with the juice of black cherries. He was taken to be hanged on Kennington Common on Monday, 3 August 1795. While being driven to the gallows he 'appeared entirely unconcerned, had a flower in his mouth...and he kept up an incessant conversation with the persons who rode beside the cart, frequently laughing and nodding to others of his acquaintances whom he perceived in the crowd which was immense.' (*Oracle and Public Advertiser*, 4 August 1795).

As he arrived at the gallows, he kicked off his boots in order to prove his mother's prophecy incorrect.

After being hanged, his body was gibbeted on Putney Common, the scene of many of his crimes, and thousands of sightseers visited the body of the last notorious highwayman, aged just twenty-two. A pamphlet published soon afterwards recounted his life. It had the no-nonsense title *Hardened Villainy Displayed*.

## John Clavell *c.*1603–42

### A royal pardon

John Clavell was descended from an ancient Dorsetshire family and the heir to Sir William Clavell, whom he later admitted he had 'grossly injured' by becoming a highwayman 'out of great necessity'.

He committed a number of robberies, on Gad's Hill and elsewhere, and was arrested in February 1626 with his companion, a soldier. In prison he wrote *A Recantation of an Ill-Led Life; or, a Discoverie of the Highway Law. With vehement Diswasions to all (in that kind) Offenders. As also, Many cautelous Admonitions and full instructions, how to know, shunne, and apprehend a Thiefe. Most necessary for all honest Travellers to peruse, observe and practise.* It was addressed pitifully 'From my lonely sad, and unfrequented chamber in the King's Bench, October 1627', and allegedly 'Approved by the King's most Excellent Majesty, and published by his express Command.' It was a grovelling apology but achieved its desired effect and he was released. However, despite an appeal signed 'Your right sorrowful Nephew', Sir William promptly disinherited him.

One of the conditions of his release was that he should serve in the army against France. This he may have done, and apparently he reformed as well, as the third edition of his 'bestselling' *Recantation* states that '...he hath also made good all these promises and resolutions'. He then vanished from history, dying, it is said, in 1642.

## John Cottington *c.*1614–59

### A Royalist highwayman

John Cottington was nicknamed 'Mull-Sack' because he was always drinking mulled sack, or sherry – especially in the Devil Tavern in Fleet Street. In early life – at the age of about eight – he had been apprenticed as a chimney sweep by his father, a drunken haberdasher of Cheapside. At the age of thirteen he ran away and took up the profession of pickpocket, becoming a great expert, but acknowledged chiefly for his Royalist sympathies. He figures in many stories in which he gets the better of the king's opponents, many of them unlikely, but all very entertaining.

It was said that he robbed Lady Fairfax, the wife of General Fairfax, of a gold watch set with diamonds, by cutting it from its chain as he politely helped her from her carriage. He narrowly escaped hanging after being caught in an attempt to rob Oliver Cromwell himself as he left Parliament. The situation was becoming awkward, and he took to the road with one Tom Cheney.

Together they once robbed Colonel Hewson, a distinguished Cromwellian, on Hounslow Heath. A troop which was following him immediately gave chase. Cottington got clean away, but Cheney was wounded, captured, condemned and hanged on the same day.

A similar fate met Captain Horne, Cottington's next companion, and he subsequently operated alone, except for large-scale hold-ups. He was outstandingly successful as a highwayman, and it was said of him that '...he constantly wore a watchmaker's and jeweller's shop in his pocket, and could at any time command a thousand pounds'.

With a handful of companions, he robbed the army pay-wagon at Shotover Hill, near Oxford, of £4,000. They caused such a commotion that the escort, thinking there was a huge band attacking them, fled in disarray.

After robbing the General Receiver at Reading of £6,000, by breaking into his house, he was captured and tried at Abingdon. Cottington was acquitted, it is said, by terrorising the jury.

He had not long been free when he killed a man called John Bridges and fled overseas. At Cologne he robbed the exiled King Charles II of plate worth £1,500 – a bizarre action, considering his former loyalty. He then appears to have entered into some strange bargain with Cromwell, involving the production of some of the King's secret papers. Perhaps, having a change of heart, he did not keep his side of the deal and back in England was imprisoned at Newgate and hanged at Smithfield Rounds in 1659.

A popular contemporary print of 'Mull-Sack' commemorates his carefree existence in the following verses:

I walk the Strand and Westminster, and scorn
To march i' the City, though I bear the horn.
My feather and my yellow band accord,
To prove me courtier: my boot, spur, and sword,
My smoking-pipe, scarf, garter, rose on shoe,
Show my brave mind t' affect what gallants do.
I sing, dance, drink, and merrily pass the day
And, like a chimney, sweep all care away.

# William Davis 1627–90

## 'The Golden Farmer'

William Davis was regarded by his friends as a successful farmer who acquired the nickname 'Golden Farmer' from his eccentric habit of paying for everything with gold.

He was born at Wrexham, now in Clwyd, but soon moved to Sudbury, where he married the daughter of a wealthy innkeeper. He established himself as a respected farmer in the Bagshot area but had a profitable sideline in highway robbery – hence his use of gold to avoid identification with the things he stole. It is said he turned to the highway in order to satisfy the demands of his large family of eighteen children. He operated on the deserted heaths on the Exeter Road (now the A30) and elsewhere, and numerous stories are told of his daring robberies.

He once held up the Duchess of Albemarle (a coarse, unpleasant woman whom Pepys calls 'Dirty Bess') on Salisbury Plain, after, it is said, single-handedly overcoming her postilion, coachman and two footmen. He took from her three diamond rings and a gold watch and scolded her for painting her face and for being niggardly.

He sometimes operated with Thomas Sympson, known as 'Old Mobb', who shares with 'Golden Farmer' the distinction of being an unusually long-lived highwayman (his career on the highway spanned an amazing forty-five years). Other stories about William Davis tell of his robbing Sir Thomas Day of £60, and of stealing back the rent money of £80 which he had just paid to his landlord by disguising himself and overtaking him on the road.

It is said that the 'Golden Farmer' retired from the road for a few years, but that he resumed his profession in the hope of making sufficient money to buy a neighbouring piece of land. He was growing old and out of practice, and he was recognised in an attempted hold-up in London. He managed to escape in Whitefriars and shot dead a butcher who pursued him. He was captured and tried at the Old Bailey sessions of 11–17 December 1690. He was condemned and hanged, probably at the end of Salisbury Court (where he had shot the butcher) on 22 December 1690, aged 64, and his body was afterwards hung in chains on Bagshot Heath. He left 'affectionate messages' for Old Mobb, who was himself hanged at Tyburn on Friday, 30 May 1691.

Much of the life and exploits of 'Golden Farmer' has been

romanticised. He was commemorated by a popular contemporary ballad called *The Golden Farmer's Last Farewell*, which was performed as a play as long afterwards as 1832. The Jolly Farmer inn at Bagshot was long called the Golden Farmer in remembrance of its notorious resident.

*William Davis is supposed to have robbed even a travelling tinker.*

# Claude Duval 1643–70

## The gallant highwayman

After Dick Turpin, Claude Duval was perhaps England's most famous highwayman. He was not English, however, having been born the son of a poor miller in Domfront, Normandy. At the age of thirteen or fourteen he went to Rouen, where he joined a group of Englishmen as a servant and accompanied them to Paris. Later he worked at the St Esprit pleasure house in the Rue de Bourchiere until he was eighteen. On the restoration of Charles II to the English throne in 1660, he accompanied a band of exiles to London, working as a footman to the Duke of Richmond.

In England, Duval got into the company of a rough crowd and became a highwayman, achieving early notoriety. A list of wanted known highwaymen published in the *London Gazette* placed him at the top, and many stories, some true, some less so, were told about his exploits.

He once stopped a coach which contained a woman and her husband – a wealthy man whom Duval knew to be carrying £400 in cash. Duval's attack was greeted with a display of indifference by the lady, who produced a flageolet and began to play a tune. Duval, entering into the spirit of the occasion, proceeded to accompany her on his own instrument, and requested permission to dance with her on the Heath – which he did expertly, in spite of his cumbersome riding boots. The romantic scene, described in Lord Macaulay's *History of England*, inspired the 1859–60 painting by William Powell Frith, now in the Manchester City Art Gallery. When Duval asked for 'payment' for the music, he was presented with £100. He was so delighted that he excused the traveller the other £300 and allowed him to continue his journey.

At the Crown Inn at Beaconsfield in Buckinghamshire, Duval overheard a farmer talking about the money he had received at Beaconsfield Fair. He bribed an ostler to dress up in cowhide and horns, and to climb down a chimney in the inn, where he created such a commotion that many customers believed it to be a visitation from the Devil himself. In the confusion Duval lifted a bag containing £100 from the farmer's pocket and rode off.

He robbed many travellers along the stretch of the Oxford Road out of London known today as the Bayswater Road, especially in the area near the Swan Inn. He became well-known and, having robbed Roper, Charles II's Master of the Buckhounds, of fifty

*The Swan, Bayswater Road, London, claims association with Claude Duval.*

guineas, he fled the country with a price on his head.

While in France he posed as an alchemist and tricked the King of France's Jesuit confessor into believing he had discovered the philosopher's stone that would turn base metal into gold. Once in his confidence, he robbed the confessor of a large amount of jewels and gold. Following this incident, he unaccountably returned to England. In London he perpetuated his reputation as a notorious highwayman, expert card-sharp, gambler and great lover for some years but was eventually captured, heavily armed but too drunk to make use of his weapons, in the Hole-in-the-Wall Tavern in Chandos Street, near the Strand.

On 17 January 1670, having been found guilty of six out of many more charges, he was sentenced to death. Many ladies pleaded for his life, but the king expressly excluded the possibility of a free

*After robbing Roper, Charles II's Master of the Buckhounds, of fifty guineas in Windsor Forest, Claude Duval was forced to flee the country.*

pardon. Duval was hanged at Tyburn on Friday, 21 January 1670. The hangman who presided, Jack Ketch, gave him no opportunity to read a speech in praise of his women friends which was later found in his pocket.

After about half an hour, his body was cut down and taken to the Tangier Tavern in St Giles, where, lit by candles, it was surrounded by a bodyguard of men in black cloaks. Huge crowds visited this dramatic lying-in-state, until a judge had to send an order to disperse them. The body was taken to St Paul's church, Covent Garden, where it was buried under the centre aisle under a stone of white marble (no longer in existence) with the epitaph:

Here lies Du Vall: Reader, if Male thou art,
Look to thy purse; if Female, to thy heart.
Much havoc has he made of both; for all
Men he made stand, and women he made fall.
The second Conqueror of the Norman race,
Knights to his arms did yield, and Ladies to his face.
Old Tyburn's Glory, England's illustrious thief,
Du Vall, the Ladies' Joy; Du Vall, the Ladies' grief.

It is said that his bones were removed and exhibited at Surgeons' Hall, but their present whereabouts are unknown.

Duval's exploits were almost immediately retold in numerous pamphlets, including 'a pindarick ode' by Samuel Butler, *To the Memory of the Most Renowned Du-Vall* (1671), and a satirical piece by Dr Walter Pope, the astronomer, entitled *The Memoires of Monsieur Du Vall* (1670), written '...as a severe reflexion on the too great fondness of English ladies toward French footmen, which at that time of day was a too common complaint'. As long as twenty-five years later, this aspect of Duval's reputation was sufficient that the conspirator Titus Oates attacked '...divers great personages of the feminine sex that on their knees made supplication for that insipid highwayman'. It was not long, though before he had achieved heroic status, inspiring numerous fictitious and highly imaginative accounts of his life – and, as in the following poem dating from 1841, his death:

A living sea of eager human faces,
A thousand bosoms, throbbing all as one,
Walls, windows, balconies, all sorts of places,
Holding their crowds of gazers to the sun:
Through the hushed groups low-buzzing murmurs run;
And on the air, with slow reluctant swell,
Comes the dull funeral-boom of old Sepulchre's bell.

Oh, joy in London now! In festal measure
Be spent the evening of this festive day!
For thee is opening now a high-strung pleasure;
Now, even now, in yonder press-yard, they
Strike from his limbs the fetters loose away!
A little while, and he, the brave Duval,
Will issue forth, serene, to glad and greet you all.

'Why comes he not? Say, wherefore doth he tarry?'
Starts the inquiry loud from every tongue.
'Surely,' they cry, 'that tedious Ordinary
His tedious psalms must long ere this have sung,—
Tedious to him that's waiting to be hung!'
But hark! old Newgate's doors fly wide apart.
'He comes, he comes!' A thrill shoots through each gazer's heart.

Joined in the stunning cry ten thousand voices,
All Smithfield answered to the loud acclaim.
'He comes, he comes!' and every breast rejoices,
As down Snow Hill the shout tumultuous came,
Bearing to Holborn's crowd the welcome fame.
'He comes, he comes!' and each holds back his breath—
Some ribs are broke, and some few scores are crushed to death.

With step majestic to the cart advances
The dauntless Claude, and springs into his seat,
He feels that on him now are fixed the glances
Of many a Briton bold and maiden sweet,
Whose hearts responsive to his glories beat.
In him the honour of 'The Road' is centred,
And all the hero's fire into his bosom entered.

His was the transport—his the exultation
Of Rome's great generals, when, from afar,
Up to the Capitol, in the Ovation,
They bore with them, in the triumphal car,
Rich gold and gems, the spoils of foreign war.
*Io Triumphe*. They forgot their clay.
E'en so Duval, who rode in glory on his way.

His laced cravat, his kids of purest yellow,
The many-tinted nosegay in his hand,
His large black eyes, so fiery, yet so mellow,
Like the old vintages of Spanish land,
Locks clustering o'er a brow of high command,

Subdue all hearts: and as, up Holborn's steep,
Toils the slow car of death, e'en cruel butchers weep.

He saw it, but he heeded not. His story,
He knew, was graven on the page of Time.
Tyburn to him was as a field of glory,
Where he must stoop to death his head sublime,
Hymned in full many an elegiac rhyme.
He left his deeds behind him, and his name—
For he, like Caesar, had lived long enough for fame.

He quailed not, save when, as he raised the chalice,—
St Giles's bowl,—filled with the mildest ale,
To pledge the crowd, on her—his beauteous Alice—
His eyes alighted, and his cheek grew pale.
She, whose sweet breath was like the spicy gale,
She whom he fondly deemed his own dear girl,
Stood with a tall dragoon, drinking long draughts of purl.

He bit his lip—it quivered but a moment—
Then passed his hand across his flushing brows;
He could have spared so forcible a comment
Upon the constancy of woman's vows.
One short sharp pang his hero-soul allows;
But in the bowl he drowned the stinging pain,
And on his pilgrimage went calmly forth again.

A princely group of England's noblest daughters
Stood on a balcony, suffused with grief,
Diffusing fragrance round them, of strong waters,
And waving many a snowy handkerchief;
Then glowed the prince of highwaymen and thief!
His soul was touched with a seraphic gleam—
That woman could be false was but a mocking dream.

.
And now, his bright career of triumph ended,
His chariot stood beneath the triple tree.
The law's grim finisher to its boughs ascended,
And fixed the hempen bandages, while he
Bowed to the throng, then bade the cart go free.
The cart rolled on, and left him dangling there,
Like famed Mohammed's tomb, uphung midway in air.

As droops the cup of the surcharged lily,
Beneath the surly buffets of the storm

Or the soft petals of the daffodilly,
When Sirius is uncomfortably warm,
So dropped his head upon his manly form,
While floated in the breeze his tresses brown.
He hung the stated time, and then they cut him down.

With soft and tender care the trainbands bore him,
Just as they found him, nightcap, rope, and all,
And placed this neat, though plain, inscription o'er him,
Among the anatomies in Surgeons' Hall,
'These are the bones of the renowned Duval.'
There still they tell us, from their glassy case,
He was the last, the best, of all that noble race.

*Hopcroft's Holt in Oxfordshire claims that Duval's ghost haunts the inn.*

59

# James Hind *c*.1618–52

## The highwayman adventurer

'Captain' James Hind was a notoriously gallant Royalist highwayman from Chipping Norton, Oxfordshire. The son of a saddler, he received a good education and, like Dick Turpin, was apprenticed to a butcher at the age of about fifteen. In less than two years he ran away, borrowed some money from his mother and made for London. He soon fell into bad company and, after causing an affray whilst drunk, found himself jailed in Poultry Compter, the sheriff's prison that stood in the City of London until 1817. There he met Thomas Allen, a highwayman with whom he joined forces on their release. Many stories, some clearly fictitious, are told of his subsequent exploits.

It is said that he won an early reputation for chivalry by returning one pound out of the fifteen he stole from a traveller on Shooter's Hill, while Allen sat astride his horse, watching proudly. There are also numerous accounts of chance meetings with Cromwell's men, of an encounter with Cromwell himself (when Allen was caught and hanged) and of robbing Hugh Peters, the regicide, in Enfield Chase, and Colonel Harrison and Serjeant Bradshaw between Shaftesbury and Sherborne. Having robbed them, Hind is said to have lectured these men about their crimes against the king. Even more fanciful are stories of his paying a poor man's debts for him and then stealing back the money from the money lender; of receiving a magic talisman from an old woman outside the George Inn, Hatfield, which protected him for three years; and of stealing a woman's £3,000 dowry, which, it is related, caused her fiancé immediately to lose interest in his bride-to-be.

His title, 'Captain', is self-assumed, but he is known to have served in the Royalist army. He received a commission from Sir William Compton and was at Colchester when it was taken by Fairfax, escaping disguised in woman's clothing, on 27 August 1648.

On 2 May 1649 he went to The Hague and then made his way to Ireland, where he became a corporal in the Marquis of Ormonde's Life Guards. He was wounded at Youghall (allegedly just as his talisman's power wore out) and escaped to Duncannon. To avoid an outbreak of the plague there, he moved to Scilly and then to the Isle of Man and on to Stirling, where he was commended by Charles II. He marched south with the king's forces, and after the

*Royalist highwayman 'Captain' James Hind robs Parliamentarian*
*Thomas Harrison on the road from Shaftesbury to Sherborne.*

defeat at the battle of Worcester (3 September 1651) he escaped to London, where he lived under the name of James Brown at a barber's shop near St Dunstan's in Fleet Street. He was betrayed and arrested on 9 November 1651 and the next day was examined by the Speaker of the House of Commons, '...in regard to his late engagement with Charles Stewart, and whether he was the man that accompanied the Scots king for the furtherance of his escape'. When asked if he had seen *Hind's Ramble* and *Hind's Exploits,* two of the many popular pamphlets about him, he replied that although they were fictitious he had played 'some merry Pranks and Revels'. He was taken to Newgate in irons, and on 12 December 1651 tried on a number of charges at the Old Bailey, where he '...deported himself with undaunted courage, yet with a civill behaviour and smiling countenance'. In the absence of conclusive evidence against him, he was remanded and sent to Reading, where on 1 March 1652 he was tried for the murder of George Sympson, a man he had shot at Knowl Hill, Maidenhead, some time before, when he mistook Sympson for a pursuer. The Act of Oblivion – an amnesty for offences committed before a certain date – came into force the next day but excluded offences against the state. Hind was duly sent to Worcester, where he was tried on a charge of high treason. Found guilty on 24 September 1652, he was hanged, drawn and quartered, and the parts of his body exhibited in different places in the town. His head, which was placed on the gate of the Severn Bridge, was subsequently removed and buried.

He died a recalcitrant Royalist and was commemorated in a very large number of 'lives' as 'The English Gusman', the 'Prince of Prigs', and as a jester and witty opponent of Cromwell. One such work, *No Jest Like a True Jest*, was said to be '...a Compendious Record of the Merry Life, and Mad Exploits of Capt. James Hind, the great Robber of England'.

## Francis Jackson d. 1674

## The recanting highwayman

Very little is known about Francis Jackson, other than what appears in his *Recantation*. Unfortunately, his repentance did not have the effect which Clavell's had almost fifty years before, and he was hanged and gibbeted for his crimes.

His early life was apparently happy, and his parents were indulgent, but after their death he was left in miserable poverty until one day he found lying in a London street a purse containing the then large sum of £10 in silver, and fifty guineas. With this he was able to equip himself as a gentleman and thus found his way into a group of young highwaymen. He escaped hanging early in his career after an incident near Barnet, by restoring what he had stolen and buying an acquittal. There is a story that he once gained the confidence of an attorney, who showed him how he concealed his money in his saddle, and subsequently robbed him between Reading and Marlborough. The table was turned on another occasion when he admitted into his band a sailor whom he had robbed and who declared that he dare not return to his wife empty-handed. The sailor later pulled out a gun and robbed Jackson of his day's takings.

On 16 March 1674, Jackson and his gang robbed the Windsor coach in broad daylight between Cranford and Hounslow, and early in the morning two days later held up two coaches in Bedfont Lane, on the Exeter Road between Hounslow and Staines. They then rode to Harrow-on-the-Hill by between 10 and 11 a.m., where they were confronted by a group of outraged armed locals. They turned and fought with more at the bottom of the hill, escaped and made their way to Paddington, Kilburn and then to Hendon and Hampstead Heath by 6 p.m., where they fought a running battle with more armed men raised by the hue and cry. There one of Jackson's companions was killed, and Jackson himself killed one Henry Miller. The highwaymen were captured and tried at the Old Bailey on 10 and 11 April and hanged on 15 April. Jackson's body was gibbeted at North End, Hampstead, on 'Gibbet Elms'.

In his cell he dictated his *Recantation* to the Reverend Samuel Smith, the Ordinary of Newgate. It was published shortly after his execution. After its superficial biography it goes on to moralise about robbery and to outline ways of avoiding being robbed. Its full wordy title is:

*Jackson's Recantation, or the Life and Death of the Notorious Highwayman now hanging in chains at Hampstead. Delivered to a Friend, a little before Execution; wherein is truly discovered the whole Mystery of that Wicked and Fatal Profession of Padding on the Road.*

His 'Confession' with those of his three companions was also published in 1674, '...being desired to be made Publick by the Persons themselves, to prevent false reports of them when they are Dead'.

## James Maclaine 1724–50

## 'The Gentleman Highwayman'

Known as 'The Gentleman Highwayman', James Maclaine was born at Monaghan in Ireland, the second son of Lauchlin Maclaine, a Presbyterian minister. His brother, Archibald Maclaine, became a well-known pastor in The Hague from 1747 to 1796. James Maclaine was well educated and was trained to be a merchant, but when he was eighteen his father died and left him an inheritance, which he immediately squandered in Dublin. His relatives disowned him and he entered the service of a gentleman, from which he was dismissed on a trip to London. He toyed with the idea of joining the army but, although the uniform appealed to him, service in Flanders did not. He soon married the daughter of a wealthy horse-dealer and keeper of the Golden Fleece in Oxford Road. He received a dowry of £500, with which he opened a grocer's and chandler's shop in Welbeck Street, and for a while lived honestly. His wife died in 1748 and, having sold his business and made provision for his two daughters, he found he had only about £85.

At this time he teamed up with an apothecary called Plunkett, and attempted, by posing as a wealthy gentleman, with Plunkett as his servant, to obtain an heiress. The project failed, and by gallivanting in society in Tunbridge Wells, Bath and London they bankrupted themselves.

Although reluctant and nervous, Maclaine stayed with Plunkett, when he decided that their only course would be to take to the road. Plunkett was always the better half of the partnership and conducted the first robbery (of £60 from a grazier) while Maclaine sat terrified on his horse. With a great sense of drama he habitually wore a Venetian mask on these occasions and gallantly, it is alleged, told ladies whom he robbed that he would accept only

*James Maclaine robbing Lord Eglinton (or 'Eglington') on Hounslow Heath, 26 June 1750: his victim's possessions were later traced back to Maclaine and he was arrested.*

what they cared to offer him.

After several successful robberies, Maclaine obtained some fine clothes and took lodgings in St James Street, a fashionable part of London, posing as an Irish squire. He soon became well-known in the West End and, with Plunkett, continued in his lucrative profession. They were said to have robbed as far afield as Chester and once to have obtained a very large sum of money from an official of the East India Company whom they met on Shooter's Hill. One moonlit night in November 1749, Maclaine robbed Horace Walpole as he returned from Holland House in Kensington to London. As he crossed Hyde Park in his carriage he was held up by Plunkett and Maclaine accidentally discharged a shot which grazed the great man's face. Maclaine was upset by this incident and wrote two letters of apology to Walpole, offering to meet him at Tyburn and to return the trinkets he had stolen from him – an offer which Walpole does not appear to have accepted.

On 26 June 1750 Maclaine and Plunkett stopped the Salisbury Flying Coach near Turnham Green and stole, among other things, an expensive waistcoat and a parcel of ribbons belonging to a Mr Higden. Later in the same day they stopped Lord Eglinton's coach

*'Newgates Lamentation or the Ladys Last Farewell of Maclean',*
*showing James Maclaine in his cell, fettered in the midst of a handful of*
*the three thousand admirers who visited him prior to his hanging on 3*
*October 1750.*

on Hounslow Heath, and Maclaine took the Lord's coat. The loss
of these clothes was advertised and Maclaine was informed upon
by a dealer to whom he attempted to sell them. He tried to lay all
blame on Plunkett, who promptly disappeared completely, but
swiftly found himself under arrest. Much excitement was caused
by this, as Maclaine was by now a well-known and popular figure
in society. Many great ladies allegedly 'shed tears in abundance'
when they visited him in his cell. He called numerous witnesses to
his good character at his trial on 13 September 1750, including
Lady Caroline Petersham, but he was found guilty and sentenced
to death. Maclaine was struck dumb by the verdict – an incident
referred to by Thomas Gray in his *Long Story*:

'A sudden fit of ague struck him,

He stood as dumb as poor Maclean.'

According to Horace Walpole, on the first Sunday after the trial
three thousand people visited him in his cell at Newgate. The crush
was so tremendous that Maclaine twice fainted. He seemed quite
disinterested about the result of the trial and all subsequent events.
He was hanged on 3 October 1750. Many chapbook 'lives' were
sold after his execution, and Soame Jenyns altered a line of his

poem, *The Modern Fine Lady,* to read:

'Some of the brightest eyes were at this time
In tears for one Maclaine.'

He was, according to the Ordinary who wrote one of the chapbook biographies:

'...in person of the middle size, well-limbed, and a sandy complexion, a broad open countenance pitted with the smallpox, but though he was called the Gentleman Highwayman and in his dress and equipage very much affected the fine gentleman, yet to a man acquainted with good breeding that can distinguish it from impudence and affectation there was very little in his address or behaviour that could entitle him to that character.'

# William Nevison 1639–84

## The Yorkshire highwayman

Described as 'the Claude Duval of the North', William Nevison – also called John, and by various other aliases – was a Yorkshire Royalist highwayman whose career is intertwined with legend.

He was born, it is related, in Pontefract in 1639. After being severely punished for stealing a silver spoon from his father, he stole about £10 from his family and, 'borrowing' the schoolmaster's horse, rode to London, killing his mount just outside the town to avoid the risk of his being identified by it. In London he worked for a brewer, from whom he stole £200, and fled to Flanders. There he joined the army under the Duke of York (later James II) and returned to England, where he became a highwayman.

There are reports of numerous robberies by Nevison – many in the true Robin Hood style, robbing only the rich and distributing a portion of his 'earnings' to the poor. He made a good living on the road, returning to his father's house in Pontefract for a while. He soon resumed his career, however, and his most notable exploit was recounted in Daniel Defoe's *A Tour thro' the Whole Island of Great Britain* (1726), where he appears as 'Mr Nicks', the hero of a legendary ride to York:

'Here it was that famous robbery was committed in the year 1676 or thereabouts; it was about four a clock in the morning when a gentleman was robbed by one Nicks on a bay mare, just on the declining part of the hill, on the west-side, for he swore to the spot and to the man. Mr Nicks who robbed him, came away to Gravesend, immediately ferried over, and, as he said, was stopped by the difficulty of the boat, and of the passage, near an hour; which was a great discouragement to him, but was a kind of bait to his horse. From thence he rode cross the county of Essex, through Tilbury, Hornden, and Bilerecay to Chelmsford. Here he stopped about half an hour to refresh his horse, and gave him some balls; from thence to Braintre, Bocking, Wethersfield; then over the downs to Cambridge, and from thence keeping still the cross roads, he went by Fenny Stanton to Godmanchester, and Huntingdon, where he baited himself and his mare about an hour; and, as he said himself, slept about half an hour, then holding on the North Road, and keeping a full larger gallop most of the way, he came to York the same afternoon, put off his boots and riding clothes, and went dressed as if he had been an inhabitant of the place, not a traveller, to the bowling-green, where, among other gentlemen, was the Lord Mayor of the city; he singling out his lordship, studied to do something particular that the Mayor might remember him by, and accordingly lays some odd bets with him concerning the bowls then running, which should cause the Mayor to remember it the more particularly; and takes occasion to ask his lordship what a clock it was; who, by pulling out his watch, told him the hour, which was a quarter before, or a quarter after eight at night. Some other circumstances, it seems, he carefully brought into the discourse, which should make the Lord Mayor remember the day of the month exactly, as well as the hour of the day.

Upon a prosecution which happened afterwards for this robbery, the whole merit of the case turned upon this singular point. The person robbed swore as above to the man, to the place, and to the time, in which the fact was committed, namely, that he was robbed on Gad's Hill in Kent, on such a day, and such a time of the day, and on such a part of the hill, and that the prisoner of the bar was the man that robbed him. Nicks, the prisoner, denied the fact, called several persons to his reputation, alleging that he was as far off as Yorkshire at the time, and that particularly the day whereon the prosecutor swore he was robbed, he was at bowls on the public green in the city of York; and to support this, he had the Lord Mayor of York to testify that he was so, and that the mayor acted so and so with him there as above.

This was so positive, and so well attested, that the jury acquitted him on a bare supposition, that it was impossible the man could be in two places so remote on one and the same day. There are more particulars related of this story, such as I do not take upon me to affirm; namely, that King Charles II prevailed on him on assurance of pardon, and that he should not be brought into any further trouble about it, to confess the truth to him privately, and that he owned to his majesty that he committed the robbery, and how he rode the journey after it, and that upon this the king gave him the name or title of Swift Nicks, instead of Nicks; but these things, I say, I do not relate as certain.'

There are many different versions of the story, and numerous highwaymen have been, at one time or another, accredited with the ride – most famously, Dick Turpin. As early as December 1668 a proclamation had offered £20 reward for the arrest of several highwaymen, including one 'Swift Nicks', and the *London Gazette* of 18 November 1669 again mentions him, adding to the confusion.

After another incident in 1676, Nevison was sentenced to deportation to Tangier, but he escaped and was imprisoned in Leicester gaol. From this place he gained his freedom once more by being carried out in a coffin – the judicious use of painted blue spots and a sleeping draught having convinced the prison authorities that he had died of the plague.

If Charles II had been delighted with Nevison earlier, he soon lost interest, as in 1681 a proclamation for his arrest was issued offering a reward of £20, and stating that he '...hath lately murdered one Fletcher, who had a warrant from a justice of peace to apprehend him'.

He was captured on 1 March 1684 by Captain Hardcastle at an inn near Wakefield and was taken to York, where he was tried. He claimed he had a royal pardon, and that the murder of Fletcher was in self defence, but he was found guilty and sentenced to death. Nevison was hanged on 15 March 1684 at the city of York's Knavesmire Gallows without Micklegate Bar. He was apparently blind drunk. A popular ballad lamented that:

He maintained himself like a gentleman
Beside he was good to the poor;
He rode about like a bold hero,
And gained himself favour therefore.

A contemporary chapbook concluded that: 'This was the end of the remarkable Mr Nevison, who was a person of quick understanding, tall in stature, every way proportionable, exceeding valiant, having also the air and carriage of a gentleman.'

# John Rann d.1774

## 'Sixteen-string Jack'

Before he became a highwayman, John Rann was a coachman to a 'gentleman of fortune near Portman Square' in London. A contemporary description informs us that he was:

'about five feet five inches high, wore his own hair, of a light brown colour, which he combed over his forehead, was remarkably clean, and particularly neat in his dress, which in two instances was very singular, that of always having sixteen strings to his breeches' knees, always of silk (by which means he acquired his fictitious name) and a remarkable hat with strings, and a button on the crown. He was straight, of gentle carriage, and makes a very handsome appearance.'

Like many before and after him, he aspired to the luxurious lifestyle of his employer but, lacking the wherewithal to obtain money honestly, turned to crime, becoming first a pickpocket with three accomplices, Jones, Clayton and Colledge. He soon graduated to highway robbery and was caught after robbing John Devall on the Hounslow Road in May 1774 but acquitted then and of other charges on several subsequent occasions during the year. His luck ran out and he was finally arrested after holding up Dr William Bell, the king's chaplain, on the Uxbridge Road, found guilty and sentenced to death. On the Sunday prior to his execution, he entertained seven girls in his cell and was said to have been in good spirits. He was hanged at Tyburn on 30 November 1774 – and immediately became a folk hero through the publication of a number of popular publications in which two of his female companions, Miss Smith and Miss Roche, provided prophetic examples of the sort of 'kiss-and-tell' journalism that is now published by tabloid newspapers.

A popular folk hero of his day, 'Sixteen-string Jack' Rann was hanged
at Tyburn a month after this portrait was engraved.

# Jack Sheppard 1702–24

## The great escaper

Jack or John Sheppard (or Shepherd – eighteenth-century spelling is inconsistent) was an all-round criminal, with highway robbery occupying only part of his nefarious activities. Through his crimes, but particularly as a consequence of his Houdini-like escapes from prison, he acquired a national reputation and was fêted as a hero while languishing in Newgate, where he sat for a portrait painted by Sir James Thornhill, one of the foremost artists of the period. Sheppard's execution at Tyburn at the age of twenty-one, which attracted a record crowd, confirmed his fame as a prominent member of the pantheon of British heroic villains. Like Dick Turpin after him, Sheppard was the subject of a bestselling novel by William Harrison Ainsworth. Sheppard's body was buried in the churchyard of St Martin-in-the-Fields, on the site of the National Gallery; his coffin was unearthed in 1866.

The following account of Sheppard's life, taken from a near-contemporary publication, *Lives of the Most Remarkable Criminals*, published in three volumes in 1735 by John Osborn of Paternoster Row, London, provides a vivid example of the sensational literature of the day.

'Amongst the prodigies of ingenious wickedness and artful mischief which have surprised the world in our time, perhaps none has made so great a noise as John Shepherd, the malefactor of whom we are now to speak. His father's name was Thomas Shepherd, who was by trade a carpenter, and lived in Spitalfields, a man of an extraordinary good character, and who took all the care his narrow circumstances would allow, that his family might be brought up in the fear of God, and in just notions of their duty towards their neighbour. Yet he was so unhappy in his children that both his son John and another took to evil courses, and both in their turns have been convicted at the bar at the Old Bailey.

After the father's death, his widow did all she could to get this unfortunate son of hers admitted into Christ's Hospital, but failing of that, she got him bred up at a school in Bishopsgate Street, where he learned to read. He might in all probability have got a good education if he had not been too soon removed, being put out to a trade, viz., that of a cane-chair-maker, who used him very well, and with whom probably he might have lived honestly. But his mother dying a short time afterwards, he was put to another, a much younger man, who used him so harshly that in a little time he ran away from him, and was put to another master, one Mr Wood in Wych Street. From his kindness and that of Mr Kneebone (whom he robbed) he was taught to write and had many other favours done by that gentleman whom he so ungratefully treated. But good usage or bad, it was grown all alike to him now; he had given himself up to all the sensual pleasures of low life. Drinking all day, and getting to some impudent and notorious strumpet at night, was the whole course of his life for a considerable space, without the least reflection on what a miserable fate it might bring upon him here, much less the judgement that might be passed upon him hereafter.

Amongst the chief of his mistresses there was one Elizabeth Lion, commonly called Edgeworth Bess, the impudence of whose behaviour was shocking even to the greatest part of Shepherd's companions, but it charmed him so much that he suffered her for a while to direct him in every thing, and she was the first who engaged him in taking base methods to obtain money wherewith to purchase baser pleasures. This Lion was a large masculine woman, and Shepherd a very little slight-limbed lad, so that whenever he had been drinking and came to her quarrelsome, Bess often beat him into better temper, though Shepherd upon other occasions manifested his wanting neither courage nor strength. Repeated quarrels, however, between Shepherd and his mistress, as it does often with people of better rank, created such coldness that they spoke not together sometimes for a month. But our robber could not be so long without some fair one to take up his time, and drive his thoughts from the consideration of his crimes and the punishment which might one day befall them.

The creature he picked out to supply the place of Betty Lion was one Mrs Maggott, a woman somewhat less boisterous in her temper, but full as wicked. She had a very great contempt for Shepherd, and only made use of him to go and steal money, or what might yield money, for her to spend in company that she liked better.

However, he still retained some affection for his old favourite, Bess Lion, who being taken up for some of her tricks, was committed to St Giles's Round-house. Shepherd going to see her there, broke the doors open, beat the keeper, and like a true knight-errant, set his distressed paramour at liberty. This heroic act got him so much reputation amongst the fair ladies in Drury Lane that there was nobody of his profession so much esteemed by them as John Shepherd, with his brother Thomas, who had taken to the same trade. Observing and being in himself in tolerable estimation with that debauched part of the sex, he importuned some of them to speak to his brother John to lend him a little money, and for the future to allow him to go out robbing with him. To both these propositions Jack (being a kind brother as he himself said) consented at the first word, and from thence forward the two brothers were always of one party. Jack having, as he impudently phrased it, lent him forty shillings to put himself in a proper plight, and soon after their being together having broke open an alehouse, where they got a tolerable booty, in a high fit of generosity, John presented it all to his brother, as, soon after, he did clothes to a very considerable extent, so that the young man might not appear among the damsels of Drury unbecoming Mr Shepherd's brother.

About three weeks after their coming together, they broke open a linendraper's shop, near Clare Market, where the brothers made good use of their time; for they were not in the house above a quarter of an hour before they made a shift to strip it of £50. But the younger brother acting imprudently in disposing of some of the goods, he was detected and apprehended, upon which the first thing he did was to make a full discovery to impeach his brother and as many of his confederates as he could. Jack was very quickly apprehended upon his brother's information, and was committed by Justice Parry to the Round-house, for further examination. But instead of waiting for that, Jack began to examine as well as he could the strength of the place of his confinement, which being much too weak for a fellow of his capacity, he marched off before night, and committed a robbery into the bargain, but vowed to be revenged on Tom who had so basely behaved himself (as Jack phrased it) towards so good a brother. However, that information going off, Jack went on in his old way as usual.

One day in May he and F. Benson being in Leicester Fields, Benson attempted to get a gentleman's watch, but missing his pull, the gentleman perceived it and raised a mob. Shepherd passing briskly to save his companion, was apprehended in his stead, and being carried before Justice Walters, was committed to New Prison, where the first sight he saw was his old companion, Bess Lion, who had found her way thither upon a like errand. Jack, who now saw himself beset with danger, began to exert all his little cunning, which was indeed his masterpiece. For this purpose he applied first to Benson's friends, who were in good circumstances, hoping by their mediation to make the matter up, but in this he miscarried. Then he attempted a slight information, but the Justice to whom he sent it, perceiving how

*Jack Sheppard posed for this portrait by royal painter Sir James Thornhill.*

trivial a thing it was, and guessing well at the drift thereof, refused it. Whereupon Shepherd, when driven to his last shift, communicated his resolution to Bess Lion. They laid their heads together the fore part of the night, and then went to work to break out, which they effected by force, and got safe off to one of Bess Lion's old lodgings, where she kept him secret for some time, frightening him with stories of great searches being made after him, in order to detain him from conversing with any other woman.

But Jack being not naturally timorous, and having a strong inclination to be out again in his old way with his companions, it was not long before he gave her the slip, and lodged himself with another of his female acquaintances, in a little by-court near the Strand. Here one Charles Grace desired to become an associate with him. Jack was very ready to take any young fellow in as a partner of his villainies, and Grace told him that his reason for doing such things was to keep a beautiful woman without the knowledge of his relations. Shepherd and he therefore getting into the acquaintance of one Anthony Lamb, an apprentice of Mr Carter, near St Clement's Church, they inveigled the young man to consent to let them in to rob his master's house. He accordingly performed it, and they took from Mr Barton, who lodged there, to a very considerable value. But Grace and Shepherd quarrelling about the division, Shepherd wounded Grace in a violent manner, and on this quarrel betraying one another, they were all taken, Shepherd only escaping. But the misfortune of poor Lamb who had been drawn in, being so very young, so far prevailed upon several gentlemen who knew him, that they not only prevailed to have his sentence mitigated to transportation, but also furnished him with all necessaries, and procured an order that on his arrival there he should not be sold as the other felons were, but that he should be left at liberty to provide for himself as well as he could.

It seems that Shepherd's gang (which consisted of himself, his brother Tom, Joseph Blake, alias Blueskin, Charles Grace, James Sikes, to whose name his companions tacked their two favourite syllables, Hell and Fury) not knowing how to dispose of the goods they had taken, made use of one William Field for that purpose, who Shepherd in his ludicrous style, used to characterise thus: that he was a fellow wicked enough to do anything, but his want of courage permitted him to do nothing but carry on the trade he did, which was that of selling stolen goods when put into his hands.

But Blake and Shepherd finding Field somewhat dilatory, not thinking it always safe to trust him, they resolved to hire a

*The celebrated escape of Jack Sheppard from the condemned cell in Newgate: Edgeworth Bess and Poll Maggott help him as Mrs Spurling keeps watch.*

warehouse and lodge their goods there, which accordingly they did, near the Horse-ferry in Westminster. There they placed what they had taken out of Mr Kneebone's house, and the goods made a great show there, whence the people in the neighbourhood really took them for honest persons, who had so great a wholesale business on their hands as occasioned their taking a place where they lay convenient for the water.

Field, however, importuned them (having got scent they had such a warehouse) that he might go and see the goods, pretending that he had it just now in his power to sell them at a very great price. They accordingly carried him thither and showed him the things. Two or three days afterwards, though he had not courage enough to rob anybody else, Field ventured to break open the warehouse, and took every rag that had been lodged there; and not long after, Shepherd was apprehended for the fact and tried at the next sessions of the Old Bailey.

When put into the condemned hold, he prevailed upon one Fowls, who was also under sentence, to lift him up to the iron spikes placed over the door which looks into the lodge. A woman of large make attending without, and two others standing behind her in riding hoods, Jack no sooner got his head and shoulders through between the iron spikes, than by a sudden spring his body followed with ease, and the women taking him down gently, he was without suspicion of the keepers (although some of them were drinking at the upper end of the lodge) conveyed safely out of the lodge door, and getting a hackney coach went clear off before there was the least notice of his escape.

However, he did not long enjoy his liberty, for strolling about Finchley Common, he was apprehended and committed to Newgate, and was put immediately in the Stone Room, where they put him on a heavy pair of irons, and then stapled him fast down to the floor. Being left there alone in the sessions time (most of the people in the gaol then attending at the Old Bailey) with a crooked nail he opened the lock, and by that means got rid of his chain, and went directly to the chimney in the room, where with incessant working he got out a couple of stones and by that means climbed up into a room called the Red Room, where nobody had been lodged for a considerable time. Here he threw down a door, which one would have thought impossible to have been done by the strength of man (though with ever so much noise); from hence with a great deal to do, he forced his passage into the chapel. There he broke a spike off the door, forcing open by its help four other doors. Getting at last upon the leads, he from thence descended gently (by the help of the blanket on which he lay, for which he went back through the whole prison) upon the leads of Mr Bird, a turner who lives next door to Newgate; and looking in at the garret window, he saw the maid going to bed. As soon as he thought she was asleep, he stepped downstairs, went through the shop, opened the door, then into the street, leaving the door open behind him.

In the morning, when the keepers were in search after him, hearing of this circumstance by the watchman, they were then perfectly satisfied of the method by which he went off. However, they were obliged to publish a reward and make the strictest enquiry after him, some foolish people having propagated a report that he had not got out without connivance. In the meanwhile, Shepherd found it a very difficult thing to get rid of his irons, being obliged to lurk about and lie hid near a village not far from town, until with much ado he fell upon a method of procuring a hammer and taking his irons off.

He was no sooner freed from the encumbrance that remained upon him, than he came secretly into the town that night, and robbed Mr Rawlin's house, a pawnbroker in Drury Lane. Here he got a very large booty, and amongst other things a very handsome black suit of clothes and a gold watch. Being dressed

*Noted escaper Jack Sheppard is at last securely manacled in Newgate.*

in this manner he carried the rest of the goods and valuable effects to two women, one of whom was a poor young creature whom Shepherd had seduced, and who was imprisoned on this account. No sooner had she taken care of the booty but he went among his old companions, pick-pockets and whores in Drury Lane and Clare Market. There being accidentally espied fuddling at a little brandy- shop, by a boy belonging to an alehouse, who knew him very well, the lad immediately gave information upon which he was apprehended, and reconducted, with a vast mob, to his old mansion house of Newgate, being so much intoxicated with liquor that he was hardly sensible of his miserable fate. However, they took effectual care to prevent a third escape, never suffering him to be alone a moment, which, as it put the keepers to a great expense, they took care to pay themselves with the money they took of all who came to see him.

On the 10th of November, 1724, he was by *Certiorari* [a writ from a superior court to a lower one] removed to the bar of the Court of King's Bench, at Westminster. An affidavit being made that he was the same John Shepherd mentioned in the record of conviction before him, Mr Justice Powis awarded judgement against him, and a rule was made for his execution on the 16th.

Such was the unaccountable fondness this criminal had for life, and so unwilling was he to lose all hopes of preserving it, that he framed in his mind resolutions of cutting the rope when he should be bound in the cart, thinking thereby to get amongst the crowd, and so into Lincoln's Inn Fields, and from thence to the Thames. For this purpose he had provided a knife, which was with great difficulty taken from him by Mr Watson, who was to attend him to death. Nay, his hopes were carried even beyond hanging, for when he spoke to a person to whom he gave what money he had remaining out of the large presents he had received from those who came to divert themselves at Shepherd's Show, or Newgate Fair, he most earnestly entreated him that as soon as possible his body might be taken out of the hearse which was provided for him, put into a warm bed, and if it were possible, some blood taken from him, for he was in great hopes that he might be brought to life again; but if he was not, he desired him to defray the expenses of his funeral, and return the overplus to his poor mother.

At the place of execution, to which he was conveyed in a cart, with iron handcuffs on, he behaved himself very gravely, confessing his robbery of Mr Philips and Mrs Cook, but denied that he and Joseph Blake had William Field in their company when they broke open the house of Mr Kneebone. After this he submitted to his fate on the 16th of November, 1724, much pitied by the mob.'

# Dick Turpin 1705–39

## The most famous of them all

'...a gay and gallant fellow, and very polite to the ladies.'
G. W. Thornbury and Edward Walford, *Old and New London*,
1873–8

'...a petty pilferer...a heartless plunderer...a brutal murderer.'
Captain L. Benson, *Remarkable Trials*, 1871

Dick Turpin became the classic highwayman, an outlaw-hero in popular imagination, quite soon after his death – to some a dashing, romantic figure, to others an unmitigated rogue. The truth lies somewhere between the two.

Turpin was born at the Rose and Crown (then the Bell Inn) at Hempstead in Essex. Both the inn and 'Turpin's Ring', a circle of oak trees opposite it, still stand, as does the church where he was baptised, son of Mary and John Turpin, a butcher. He received an adequate schooling (he was by no means the illiterate oaf he is sometimes made out to be) under James Smith, the local schoolmaster, and was apprenticed to a butcher in Whitechapel at the age of about sixteen. He married Betty Millington, Smith's father's maid, and was established as a butcher in Thaxted by 1728. After a short stay at Enfield, he set up as a butcher in Sewardstone, where, in 1733, he fell into debt and resorted to stealing cattle from a Mr Giles of Plaistow. He was traced by their hides, but eluded his pursuers, taking shelter in the Rodings area of Essex. He found his way into a gang of smugglers working near Canvey Island and then joined a group of deer-stealers – at that time a capital offence. His next criminal activity was that of housebreaking with the notorious Gregory's gang in the lonely rural areas of Essex, Kent and Surrey.

The gang became so troublesome that a proclamation was issued, offering a reward of £50 for the arrest of any member. Some were subsequently captured, and Turpin himself was mentioned briefly in the newspaper accounts of the gang's operations. In the *London Gazette* of February 1735 he was described thus:

'Richard Turpin, a Butcher by Trade, is a Tall Fresh Coloured Man, very much marked with the Small Pox, about 26 years of age, about five feet nine inches High, lived some time ago in Whitechapel and did lately lodge somewhere about Millbank, Westminster, wears a Blue Grey Coat and a Light Natural Wig.'

81

*The oak trees known as 'Turpin's Ring' and his birthplace in Hempstead, Essex.*

Gregory, the leader of the gang, was soon caught, hanged and gibbeted, and the remaining members dispersed. Turpin lay low in east London for a while, and then entered history as a highwayman. His first robbery was announced in July 1735 and undertaken in the company of one Rowden. Parting from him, Turpin began to operate alone in Essex. It is related that one day he held up another highwayman, Robert King. When King announced his identity, the pair entered on a successful partnership, robbing horsemen and carriages around London and as far afield as Ipswich. It is generally supposed that it was William Harrison Ainsworth's once popular novel *Rookwood* (1834) that established Turpin as a kind of folk hero. In fact, although it clearly gave wide currency to many legends about him, including the (totally untrue) ride to York and stories of the equally apocryphal Black Bess, the 'wonder horse', tales were already circulating by this time, and numerous 'lives' were published between his death and 1834, some going into several editions. In the belief of Lord Macaulay Turpin just happened to be the right sort of character to romanticise; if it had not been him, some other eighteenth-century highwayman would have done equally well.

In any event, with true and spurious stories circulating about his activities, Turpin found things getting hot. He and King could not hide in inns as landlords feared the loss of their licences more than the threats of a couple of rogues, and so they hid in Epping Forest – then considerably larger and denser than today – where they were fed by Turpin's long-suffering wife, Betty. Reports of their expeditions to the highroads of Essex continued, but they managed to escape detection by riding to their hideout, using such curious devices as circular horseshoes to confuse their pursuers.

They robbed gamblers returning from Newmarket, and from a Mr Major they stole both money and his horse, a well-known thoroughbred racer called White Stockings. The irate Mr Major reported the incident to Dick Bayes, landlord of the Green Man, Epping, who suggested that Mr Major issue posters announcing his loss. This he did, and the horse was soon traced to the Red Lion Inn, Whitechapel. An attempt was made to arrest Robert King, and Turpin, riding up, apparently shot and killed King's brother Matthew quite by accident. In the ensuing confusion Dick Bayes wounded Robert King, and he subsequently died in jail. Turpin fled but was on this occasion traced to his hideout by Thomas Morris, a forest keeper. Cornered, Turpin shot Morris dead and was forced to hide in a tree for some time to evade the hue and cry. He moved to Huntingdonshire, then returned to London. He apparently had a number of narrow escapes, and various confused stories circulated concerning his whereabouts – some even declaring that he had been captured and jailed.

Of course, by this time Turpin was widely known and easily recognisable, but he was also adept at his profession and continued to hold up coaches and constantly managed to foil the law's attempts to capture him. So great was the public outcry for action that eventually a proclamation was posted offering £200 – a very large sum of money – for his arrest. Nevertheless, he remained free, taking time off from his work only, it would seem, to visit the hundreds of inns which proclaim some association with him.

In July 1737 Turpin went to Long Sutton, Lincolnshire, where he lived under an assumed name. In those days, communications were poorly developed, and it was quite some time before it was rumoured that he had been spotted at the races. From Long Sutton he travelled to Welton in Yorkshire, living under the name of John Palmer (Palmer was his mother's maiden name) as an ostensibly respectable cattle- and horse-dealer. A complaint was lodged against him, however, on a trivial matter: he had – probably whilst drunk – shot a fowl belonging to his landlord. Investigations revealed that he had indulged in certain suspicious activities in Lincolnshire, and he was jailed in York Castle. He wrote to his brother-in-law requesting references as to his good character, but the letter was by chance seen by James Smith, the schoolmaster who had taught Turpin to write, and who instantly recognised the handwriting of his now infamous pupil. Mr Smith went to York and identified 'John Palmer' as Dick Turpin, and, though a trial followed, it was clear that Turpin's fate was sealed. The account of his execution, apart from mentioning that he was 'the notorious Highwayman Turpin' is very matter-of-fact about the affair, but then who, on Saturday 7 April 1739, could imagine the place Dick Turpin would find in history?

'The notorious Richard Turpin, and John Stead, were executed at York for Horse-stealing. Turpin behaved in an undaunted Manner; as he mounted the Ladder, feeling his right leg tremble, he stamp'd it down, and looking round about him an with unconcerted Air, he spoke a few words to the Topsman, then threw himself off, and expir'd in five Minutes. He declared himself to be the notorious Highwayman Turpin, and confess'd a great Number of Robberies, and that he shot the Man that came to apprehend him on Epping Forest, and King, his own Companion, undefignedly, for which latter he was very sorry. He gave £3 10s. to 5 Men who were to follow the Cart as Mourners, with Hatbands and Gloves, to them and several others. He was bury'd in St George's Churchyard in a neat Coffin, with this inscription, J. P. 1739. R. T. aged 28. The Mob having got Scent that his Body was stole away to be anatomized, went to the Place, and brought it away almost naked on Mens Shoulders, and filling the Coffin with Lime, bury'd it in the same Grave.

He was first apprehended for stealing a Game Cock at Welton, near Brough in Yorkshire, where he had lived since the Proclamation against him under the Name of John Palmer, by dealing in Horses, which he sold to Gentlemen who he used to hunt with.'

Dick Turpin's obituary from the<br>
Gentleman's Magazine, 1739

Turpin soon attained the legendary stature he has held ever since, hailed in fiction and poetry as one of the greatest of all British heroes, and even in parodies, such as the Miltonian *To the Hero of 'Rookwood'* (1841) by 'Jack Fireblood':

Turpin! thou shouldst be living at this hour!
England hath need of thee: common and fen,
Hounslow and Bagshot, tavern, boozing-ken,
The triple tree, and stone jug's lonely bower,

Have forfeited their ancient English dower
Of dashing Tobygloaks*. We are sneaks, not men.
Oh! raise us up, return to us again.
And give us will to take a purse and power!
Thy soul from vulgar filchers dwelt apart:
Thou hadst a steed, whose hoofs devoured the lea;
Under the midnight heavens, majestic, free,
Thou tookst the air on the King's common way,
Whistling serenely, and, with regal air,
The lieges under tribute oft didst lay.

*Tobygloaks = highwaymen.

Turpin was the subject of Edward Viles's *Black Bess, or the Knight of the Road*, a 'penny dreadful' that appeared weekly for almost five years during the 1860s. Black Bess achieved independent fame of her own, appearing in such tragic verses as the anonymous *My Poor Black Bess*:

When fortune, blind goddess, she fled my abode,
Old friends proved ungrateful, I took to the road;
To plunder the wealthy to aid my distress,
I bought thee to aid me, my poor Black Bess.

When dark sable night its mantle had thrown
O'er the bright face of nature, how oft we have gone
To famed Hounslow Heath, though an unwelcome guest
To the minions of fortune, my poor Black Bess.

How silent thou stood when a carriage I've stopped,
And their gold and their jewels its inmates I've dropped;
No poor man I plundered or e'er did oppress
The widow or orphan, my poor Black Bess.

When Argus-eyed justice did me hotly pursue,
From London to York like lightning we flew;
No toll-bar could stop thee, thou the river didst breast,
And in twelve hours reached it, my poor Black Bess.

But fate darkens o'er us, despair is my lot,
The law does pursue us, through a cock which I shot;
To save me, poor brute, thou didst do thy best,
Thou art worn out and weary, my poor Black Bess.

Hark the bloodhounds approach, they never shall have

85

A beast like thee, noble, so faithful and brave;
Thou must die, my dumb friend, though it does me distress,
There, there, I have shot thee, my poor Black Bess.

And in after ages, when I'm dead and gone,
This tale will be handed from father to son,
My fate some may pity, but all will confess,
'Twas in kindness I killed thee, my poor Black Bess.

No one can say that ingratitude dwelt
In the bosom of Turpin, 'twas a vice he ne'er felt;
I shall die like a man, and soon be at rest,
Then farewell for ever, my poor Black Bess.

*Dick Turpin's grave at York: after being hanged, his body was rescued from being dissected and was buried in St George's churchyard.*

# FURTHER READING

Anonymous. *Lives of the Most Remarkable Criminals.* 1735 (reprinted 1927).

Dash, Arty, and Day, Julius E. *Immortal Turpin: The Authentic History of England's Most Notorious Highwayman.* 1948.

Harper, Charles G. *Half-hours with the Highwaymen.* 1908.

Hibbert, Christopher. *Highwaymen.* 1967.

Hibbert, Christopher . *The Road to Tyburn: Jack Sheppard and the 18th Century Underworld.* 1957.

Knapp, A., and Baldwin, W. (editors). *The Newgate Calendar.* 1828.

Pringle, Patrick. *Stand and Deliver: The Story of the Highwayman.* 1951.

Stockman, Rocky. *The Hangman's Diary.* 1993.

Williams, Brian. *Stand and Deliver.* Hillingdon Borough Libraries, 1986.

# INDEX